THE IMPACT OF POPULATION CHANGE ON BUSINESS ACTIVITY IN RURAL AMERICA

D1519401

Other Titles in This Series

†Available in hardcover and paperback.

Rural Studies Series

The Impact of Population Change on Business Activity in Rural America
Kenneth M. Johnson

Dr. Johnson moves beyond the existing literature on rural-urban population shifts during the past forty years to examine the effects of those shifts on the business infrastructure that supplies goods and services to rural areas in the United States. First establishing a historical demographic context to serve as a backdrop, he provides a detailed longitudinal treatment on the linkage between population change and the rural commercial infrastructure, as well as timely information on the impact of the recent rural population turnaround on business. Some of his findings, based on the latest data available, refute earlier expectations that a decrease in population necessarily leads to a decline in the local business community.

Kenneth M. Johnson is an associate professor in the Department of Sociology at Loyola University of Chicago, where he teaches courses in demography, research methods, and statistics. Most of his research has focused on nonmetropolitan demographic trends and their impact on the local economic and organizational structure. Dr. Johnson is also a principal member of the Applied Demographic Research Group, which does demographic consulting for large corporations, including McDonald's and Budget Rent a Car.

THE IMPACT OF
POPULATION CHANGE
ON BUSINESS ACTIVITY
IN RURAL AMERICA

Kenneth M. Johnson

Westview Press / Boulder and London

Rural Studies Series, Sponsored by the Rural Sociological Society

This is a Westview softcover edition, manufactured on our own premises using equipment and methods that allow us to keep even specialized books in stock. It is printed on acid-free paper and bound in softcovers that carry the highest rating of NASTA in consultation with the AAP and the BMI.

Published in 1985 in the United States of America by Westview Press, Inc., 5500 Central Avenue, Boulder, Colorado 80301; Frederick A. Praeger, Publisher

Library of Congress Cataloging in Publication Data
Johnson, Kenneth M. (Kenneth Michael), 1950–
    The impact of population change on business activity
in rural America.
    (Rural studies series / sponsored by the Rural
Sociological Society)
    Includes bibliographies and index.
    1. United States—Population, Rural. 2. Store
location—United States. 3. Retail trade—United
States—Location. I. Title. II. Series: Rural studies
series of the Rural Sociological Society.
    HB2385.J64 1985   381'.1'0973   84-26962
    ISBN 0-86531-584-1 (soft : alk. paper)

Composition for this book was provided by the authors
Printed and bound in the United States of America

10   9   8   7   6   5   4   3   2   1

To Brenda

Contents

Tables and Figures

Figures

Foreword

This book examines the implications of population change for the organization of business activity in the rural United States. Its main contribution lies in its examination of a complex set of linkages between population change on the one hand, and the commercial organization of rural society on the other over an extended period of history. It is an example of how demographic research can be applied to real-life situations in a broad societal context.

The book is rooted in sociological human ecology, a basic tenet of which is that population change cannot occur for any significant period of time without resultant adjustments in the social organization of society. Dr. Johnson attempts to explain not only the mechanisms of this process but also its implications.

The research reported here focuses on three main issues: (1) What is the historical pattern of demographic change in the rural United States? (2) How have these demographic shifts influenced business infrastructure? (3) How has the historical linkage between population change and business change been affected by the recent population turnaround in the rural United States? The research demonstrates that population change does have a significant impact on local business activity, but the linkage is complex and adjustment is accomplished only after a considerable length of time. The research also shows that the recent resurgence of rural population growth has stimulated a business renaissance. In fact, some rural communities now have business growth rates that equal or exceed those in metropolitan areas.

Demographers will find this study of significant value because of its focus on the consequences of population change and its application of the human ecological perspective. Rural researchers will find the specific focus on business infrastructure and activity an important adjunct to broader work that has been done on rural demographic and economic change. And business planners will gain insights into the vast and expanding market for goods and services that continues to exist outside of metropolitan areas in small towns and villages and in the open country.

David L. Brown
Chairman, Board of Editors
Rural Studies Series

Preface

Nonmetropolitan areas of the United States have changed a great deal in the sixty years spanned by this research. In 1920, half the population resided in areas now considered nonmetropolitan, but in the following years millions left, attracted by the economic and social opportunities of the nation's urban centers. By 1970, less than a quarter of the population lived in nonmetropolitan areas. The rural-to-urban migration stream that underlay this phenomenon was among the most enduring trends of U.S. demographic history. Yet the final decade of this study witnessed a remarkable population renaissance in nonmetropolitan areas. Counties with long histories of population decline began to grow, and nonmetropolitan growth rates exceeded those in metropolitan areas for the first time in at least a century. Scholars understand many of the reasons for the protracted nonmetropolitan decline and have some idea of the causes of the recent nonmetropolitan turnaround. What is not well understood is the long-term consequences such population trends have for the organizational structure serving nonmetropolitan residents.

This research moves beyond the existing literature on twentieth-century nonmetropolitan population shifts to examine the consequences of such shifts for the business infrastructure providing goods and services to nonmetropolitan residents. The book focuses on retailing and service delivery because the need to serve a proximate clientele makes the business infrastructure acutely sensitive to local population shifts. My primary interest throughout is in the long-term influence of population change, not in short-term fluctuations. Information about how the business infrastructure responds to population change will be useful to others examining the linkages among components of the ecological complex, as well as to planners and researchers concerned specifically with the people and businesses of nonmetropolitan areas.

I generally use the term *nonmetropolitan* in preference to *rural,* but have occasionally used the two terms interchangeably for variety. In the few instances where *rural* and *nonmetropolitan* are used in distinct senses, those senses will be evident from the context.

Except where another source is explicitly stated, all the data presented in the tables and figures come from one of the products of the Bureau of the Census. Most of the census data were obtained through the Inter-University Consortium for Political and Social Research in Ann Arbor, Michigan.

I am grateful to many people for their contribution to this project. David Brown has been unflagging in his support and encouragement, and he took the time to read and comment on the entire manuscript. Amos Hawley helped me to clarify my thoughts on the theoretical aspects of this study and gave freely of his time and knowledge, as did Ross L. Purdy, who originally stimulated my interest in the topic. Other colleagues who took time from their busy schedules to read parts of what eventually became this manuscript include Michael Welch, Kirsten Gronbjerg, William Bates, John S. Reed, John Kasarda, John Florin, and Peter Uhlenberg. I have also been fortunate to have the help of several excellent research assistants through the years, including Kelly Krafft-Blum, Marilyn Fernandez, Shobha Srinivasan, James Lucas, and Dennis Pedrelli. The demanding task of typing the manuscript and tables fell to Pat Pierce and Dorothy Blumenthal. Nancy Mann's editorial work has done much to improve the final manuscript. Finally, I owe a debt of gratitude I can never properly express to my wife, Brenda, for her continued support and encouragement.

Kenneth M. Johnson

THE IMPACT OF POPULATION CHANGE ON BUSINESS ACTIVITY IN RURAL AMERICA

1
Introduction

The recent resurgence of population gain in the nonmetropolitan United States raises many questions about the implications such population change has for the institutions and organizations serving rural people. Unfortunately, efforts to answer these questions highlight serious gaps in our understanding of the linkages between population change and other systemic components. This book examines the impact of population change on the businesses providing nonmetropolitan residents with retail goods and services.

The phrase "rural business" may still bring to mind visions of a rustic crossroads general store and the Sears catalog. But today, rural business is big business, providing more than 200 billion dollars of goods and services annually to nearly 58 million nonmetropolitan residents. And in recent years nonmetropolitan business gains have exceeded those in the traditionally faster growing metropolitan business sector. Certainly the nonmetropolitan population renaissance has been an important factor in such gains, but the relationship between population change and business change is only vaguely understood.

This research moves beyond the existing literature on rural-urban population shifts during the past half century to examine the impact such population shifts have had on the business infrastructure that supplies goods and services to rural areas. It does so by establishing a historical demographic context to serve as a backdrop and then providing a detailed longitudinal treatment of the linkage between population change and the rural commercial infrastructure. Recent business patterns in nonmetropolitan areas can be understood only in the context of the demographic, economic, and social trends that have swept rural areas during the past century.

Study Overview

At the most general level, this study investigates the dynamics of system change. It seeks to determine what effect population change has on the organizational structure developed to provide the proximate population with many of its material necessities. Its basic theoretical framework is that of human ecology, one of whose basic tenets holds that change in one component of the ecological complex cannot long prevail without concomitant adjustments in other ecological components. This book focuses on how the organizational component of the ecological complex responds to changes in the size of the local population.

I have chosen to concentrate specifically on retail and service establishments in nonmetropolitan counties, partly to keep the project within practical limits, but also because much of the organizational adjustment to population change occurs at geographic levels greater than the county. My focus here is on those organizational components that, because they provide the population with its most frequently needed goods and services, are most likely to reflect the localized effects of population change.

The unit of analysis throughout is the U.S. county. The boundaries of such places have remained relatively stable over time, and counties are large enough to encompass much of the economic activity of their resident populations. I have included all counties beyond the boundaries of the nation's metropolitan centers as of 1974, in order to avoid the complications that arise from intermingling rural and urban counties. In addition, nonmetropolitan counties are more numerous than their metropolitan counterparts and have as a group experienced a more heterogeneous pattern of population change.

The study spans the period from 1930 to 1982, and its primary concern is with the effect of extended population change. Minor, short-term population shifts are not of interest here because the organizational structure is sufficiently flexible to tolerate short-term fluctuations without fundamental readjustment. On the other hand, any organizational readjustment to population change lasting ten years or longer is assumed to be permanent rather than temporary. One would expect the most substantial organizational adjustments in the numerous counties with protracted histories of consistent population change, some of which span fifty years.

Principal Research Foci

My analytic strategy is organized around three major research questions:

1. What patterns of demographic and population change predominated in the nonmetropolitan United States between 1930 and 1970?
2. How did the organizational structure providing goods and services to nonmetropolitan residents respond to the population shifts common between 1930 and 1970?
3. How has the local nonmetropolitan business infrastructure been affected by the rural population turnaround since 1970?

This analytic strategy allows for a detailed review of historical demographic trends, in order to provide a context for examining the longitudinal impact of population change on the delivery of retail goods and services to nonmetropolitan residents. The post-1970 era is examined separately because recent nonmetropolitan demographic trends reflect a fundamental break from those of the preceding century. Finally, the focus on the impact of the nonmetropolitan population renaissance on the commercial infrastructure allows for a comparison of historical and contemporary trends.

Population as an Independent Variable

In ecological research, population is not generally considered to be an independent variable (Hawley, 1973). Rather, ecol-

ogists believe, changes in population occur in response to
changes in the organizational structure of a system or, much
less frequently, as a result of drastic environmental change.
In this view population cannot initiate change, and acts
essentially as a dependent variable.

This study is not intended to address the question of
whether it is possible for population to initiate change. Obviously the population change in nonmetropolitan counties
during this century was a response to antecedent changes
in the organizational and environmental structure of the
country. Still, the causal linkages among components of the
ecological complex are not unidirectional. A change initiated
in one segment of the structure may, after reverberating
through the system, eventually require additional change in
the originating segment. Because my primary interest is in
the linkage between two components of the ecological complex,
the original source of the change is immaterial. The fact that
population change was caused by prior organizational change
does not negate its role as an independent variable affecting
the retail and service sectors of the organizational structure.
Because these sectors are heavily dependent on the patronage
of local residents, any significant shift in the size or composition
of the local population will require organizational readjustments. Thus, for my purposes, population change may appropriately be used as an independent variable.[1]

The Nonmetropolitan County as Unit of Analysis

In order to delineate the impact of population change one
must choose a unit of analysis that is amenable to study over
time. In selecting a unit of analysis, I have used the following
criteria:

1. A large database spanning the period under study must
   be available for the unit.
2. The geographic boundaries of the unit must remain
   stable over the period studied.
3. The unit should be of sufficient size to capture most of
   the retail and service activities of households within it.

The need for a large body of data collected over an extended period of time limited the usable units to those available from official sources. In short, the selection came down to determining which administratively defined entity conformed most closely to the stated criteria.

Counties have shown remarkable geographic stability over time and are used in the collection of a great deal of data. It is true that counties lack autonomy and are, therefore, better thought of as subsystems rather than systems. As with any other subsystem, a county has permeable boundaries, and though it may be a very productive and important part of the parent system, it is not self-sufficient. Thus, it is unreasonable to assume that either the original causes of population shifts or the organizational changes stimulated by them are restricted to the geographic boundaries of the county.

There is little question that interaction occurs across county lines. The point at issue is whether there is enough such movement to damage the usefulness of the county as a unit of analysis. The effect of population change is experienced along a gradient, with the intensity of the effect decreasing as distance increases. By choosing the county as the appropriate unit of analysis, one imposes an artificial set of boundaries on this gradient and assumes that it is steep enough so that most of the activity occurs within the county. To the extent that this is not the case, the impact of population change on the organizational structure will be underestimated.

This difficulty is lessened somewhat if one recognizes that the permeability of subsystem boundaries varies from function to function. The higher the frequency of interaction between units, the more likely they are to be in close physical proximity. Therefore, by limiting attention to functions households require often, one can maximize the probability of proximity and minimize the effect of permeable county boundaries.[2]

Retail and service goods are certainly among the most frequently required of all functions. Although there have been few studies of where nonmetropolitan residents do most of their daily business, those available suggest that a significant amount of that business is carried out within the county of residence. In a study of a rural Nebraska county, Anderson

(1961) found the radius for shopping and related services to be about fifteen miles, which is roughly the radius of a Midwestern county. He also noted that 78 percent of the farm population he studied reported that the town they visited most was in their county of residence.[3] County seats are centers of local shopping activity as well as providers of governmental and related services (Anderson, 1961; Fuguitt, 1965c; Voss, 1980). In short, using the county to collapse the demand radii for a variety of services and household goods into a single unit of analysis will introduce some error, but one can minimize it by limiting attention to retail and service functions.

The county has enjoyed a long history of use as a unit of analysis in research of this kind (Frisbie and Poston, 1975, 1978; Beale, 1964, 1969, 1974, 1978; Beale and Fuguitt, 1975; Bollinger, 1972; Zelinsky, 1962). Although the use of counties has been criticized, (Fox and Kumar, 1965), it does appear to be most appropriate for this study. Given the mobility provided by modern means of transportation, areal units such as towns or minor civil divisions are simply too small. Even the county may be slightly too small to encompass the demand radii for the entire range of daily business activities, but the state economic area, the next highest level of aggregation, is certainly too large. The county is the best compromise among the available administrative entities, and in addition has been a very stable geographic unit through time. Finally, the large volume of data collected for counties through the years makes them amenable to longitudinal study.

Study Population

The study population for this project includes nearly all U.S. counties not within one of the 243 Standard Metropolitan Statistical Areas designated by the Bureau of the Census in 1974. Although the technical definition of an SMSA is rather complex, it generally includes a central city of at least 50,000 and the county in which the city is located. Adjacent counties are included if they meet certain criteria of social and economic integration with the central city county.[4] This definition of nonmetropolitan counties is consistent with those used in earlier research on the same topic (Beale and Fuguitt, 1975; Hines, Brown, and Zimmer, 1975). The study population includes 2,425 nonmetropolitan counties in the continental United States.[5]

Linkages Between Population Change and the Local Business Infrastructure

Surprisingly little research has been done on the relationship between population change and the local business structure. At the county level, the few studies that exist are limited in scope and often focus on a single county. Studies of towns or villages are more numerous, but the generalizability of findings from such small areal units to the county level is limited at best. Despite these shortcomings, empirical evidence links population and business change.

The Impact of Population Change

Comparative cross-sectional research on nonmetropolitan counties demonstrates that population change exerts a strong causal impact on the retail structure serving an area (Johnson, 1982a). Retail gains are greatest in counties with protracted population gain. In contrast, in counties subjected to sustained population decline, retailing either grows slowly or stagnates. Additional evidence suggests that the recent resurgence of widespread population increase in nonmetropolitan areas is stimulating a retail boom in many rural parts of the country (Johnson, 1982b).

Johansen and Fuguitt (1979, 1984) have also found that population change exerts a strong influence on the business structure of rural villages. Their important studies represent the first nationwide research on business trends in rural villages since the pioneering work of Brunner and his associates (Brunner et al., 1927; Brunner and Kolb, 1933; Brunner and Lorge, 1937). Johansen and Fuguitt's work confirms earlier fragmentary evidence that sustained population increase stimulates the local business structure, whereas population decline causes it to stagnate or decline (Adams, 1969; Bollinger, 1972; Raup, 1961). In declining counties, retailers specializing in high-cost shopping goods are hit hardest (Bollinger, 1972). Among such retailers, losses resulting from population decline are aggravated by the increased mobility, affluence, and sophistication of the remaining residents, as well as by the market encroachments of high-volume chain competitors located in large places (Anderson, 1961; Campbell, 1975; Doeksen et al., 1974).

Several authors, using population change in the traditional way, as a dependent variable, have found that population gains are common in areas where the provision of retail and other services is a major sustenance activity (Frisbie and Poston, 1975; 1978; Fuguitt and Deeley, 1966; Hansen, 1973; Hassinger, 1957a; Tarver, 1972). Consumer spending in such areas stimulates the local economy, creating jobs and slowing the tide of outmigration (Hansen, 1973). These established retail centers are also favored sites for new firms, which enhance the areas' growth potential even further. In contrast, areas without extensive retail and service facilities lose population (Frisbie and Poston, 1978). Although the causal ordering of population and retail change in these studies is not consistent with that used here, these works do confirm a positive association between the variables.

The reaction of business to population shifts is complex. For example, the loss of rural population resulting from farm consolidation and mechanization reduces the demand for day-to-day goods such as groceries (Raup, 1961; Bollinger, 1972). At the same time, the increased affluence of the remaining population, coupled with the technological and financial requirements of commercial farming, increases the demand for durable goods and specialized services. Such demand shifts increase the chances of survival for large places that can generate enough volume to support specialized retail and service functions (Bollinger, 1972; Fuguitt, 1965b). Small places' lack of adequate banking facilities to meet the needs of modern agriculture further hinders them in their competition with larger places offering better financial services (Hansen, 1973; Ellenbogen, 1974). There is also limited evidence of a decrease in medical and dental personnel in population loss areas (Doerflinger and Robinson, 1962).

The impact of population change reaches beyond the business infrastructure to affect the provision of public as well as private services. The shrinkage of the local tax base resulting from outmigration and small business failures harms an array of other services. Educational opportunities in particular are acutely sensitive to population change. Although some flexibility exists, there are minimum population floors below which it is extremely difficult to provide adequate educational services. When district size falls below such minimums, essential services and programs are generally cut (White and Tweenten, 1973). This problem is often exacerbated by local resistance to school district consolidation, despite the increased efficiency and enriched curriculum it would produce (Klietsch, 1962). Inadequate population size also makes it difficult to maintain adequate levels of police and fire protection, water distribution, waste disposal, electricity, and road maintenance. Inability to provide adequate services precipitates further population decline, because without adequate services towns are unable to attract new industries (Campbell, 1975). In short, a snowball effect develops, with an initial period of population loss placing the local area at a competitive disadvantage, thereby increasing the likelihood of later decline (Taves, 1961).

Local Response to Population Change

The adjustment of the local business infrastructure to population change is also affected by the reaction of local residents. Although much of this response is psychological, past research suggests that local reactions to population shifts are also manifested in structural adjustments.

Prolonged population decline generates a variety of reactions from the remaining population. Prominent among these are a resistance to any reduction in the local availability of functions, and a risk avoidance style of management premised on the conservation of available resources rather than innovation (Taves, 1961; Klietsch, 1962; Rust, 1975). Such psychological factors have organizational consequences. For example, some proprietors resist closing their establishments despite dwindling profits because they cannot recover the capital invested and have few alternative employment prospects. The conservative management styles that pervade business in declining areas only perpetuate decline, because often bold action offers the only chance to break the cycle (Adams, 1969). Areas subjected to prolonged decline may develop a pervasive, debilitating climate of despair, with the local population feeling powerless to stem the decline (Rundbald, 1957; Taves, 1961).

Not everyone in a rural area desires unbridled growth and prosperity. Some local businessmen fear the competition growth might bring, including chain stores that might break their monopoly on retail trade and new industry that might upset the local wage structure (Simon and Gagon, 1967). Recent studies of the population turnaround also suggest that there is resistance to efforts to expand the service delivery system to meet the demands of a growing population (Daily and Campbell, 1980; Ploch, 1980). Residents fear that certain types of retail and service outlets will change the rural atmosphere they cherish. Often such resistance is reflected in restrictive zoning and building regulations that limit the possibilities for business expansion.

Other Factors Affecting the Local Business Infrastructure

Efforts to delineate the impact of population change on the local retail and service structure are complicated by other factors, including the increased mobility of rural residents, the rising affluence and changing lifestyle of the nonmetropolitan population, and the changing character of business operations. The interaction of these factors amplifies the impact of population change on local businesses.

As farm income increased and rural and urban life styles converged, the nonmetropolitan population came to expect the variety and ready availability of goods and services formerly provided only in large urban centers (Anderson, 1961). There was an increased demand for newer forms of retail establishments such as department stores, discount centers, and supermarkets. The extent to which such establishments are now commonplace in nonmetropolitan areas is witnessed by the penetration of discount centers and supermarkets into even the low population density areas of the Midwest (Campbell, 1975; Johnson 1982*b*).

As business responded to shifting nonmetropolitan consumer demands, the changing economies of scale raised the minimum revenue thresholds necessary to remain in business. Although rising nonmetropolitan incomes provided some of the needed revenue, expanding rural establishments also had to enlarge their geographic market areas to reach enough customers (Doeksen et al., 1974). The number of patrons required to support a given business has risen steadily through the past several decades (Johansen and Fuguitt, 1973, 1979, 1984).

Population decline areas and those counties without a large town were most likely to suffer in the competition among businesses, because larger, growing nonmetropolitan centers were favored sites for new or expanded establishments. Such centers offered a proximate population of some size, and, because other retailers were already present, offered agglomeration advantages likely to attract more customers. The result has been a centralization of functions, with small places providing convenience goods, but no longer able to compete favorably with large centers in the provision of specialized retail goods or services (Fuguitt, 1965*c*; Bollinger, 1972). Functions increasingly found only in large urban centers include banks, specialized health care personnel, machine repair shops, farm equipment dealers, auto dealers, and secondary schools (Raup, 1961; Bollinger, 1972; Brown, 1974; Fuguitt, 1965*b*). Extensive retail and service facilities enhance the growth possibilities for a town or county, and the lack of such facilities in small, declining areas further increases the likelihood of additional population loss.

Expansion of scale would not have been possible without substantial improvements in the nonmetropolitan transportation system. Automobiles and good roads allowed rural residents to travel farther to patronize larger, more competitive outlets (Campbell, 1975; Bollinger, 1972; Doeksen et al., 1974).

The greater mobility of the rural population, together with its rising affluence and more sophisticated consumer expectations, increased the proportion of shopping that was done in larger regional shopping centers. Such access to distant centralized shopping facilities, in turn, contributed significantly to the decline of retail activities in smaller centers (Raup, 1961; Anderson, 1961; Campbell, 1975; Bollinger, 1972). Farm equipment, automobiles, and specialized medical services were among the items rural residents were willing to travel some distance to obtain (Bollinger, 1972; Brown, 1974). County seats were popular centers for shopping as well as a variety of other activities (Anderson, 1961; Fuguitt, 1965*c*; Voss, 1980).

The retail sectors of small towns near larger places suffered most. Such small towns tended to have fewer locally available functions than similar small towns distant from larger centers (Hassinger, 1957*b*; Hodge, 1965; Johansen and Fuguitt, 1973, 1979). Medical services were also less available in smaller places, if there was a larger place nearby (Hassinger and McNamara, 1956). Although most research on this topic has been applied to towns, there is little question that it is also relevant to counties.

Summary

The existing literature indicates that population change does exert a strong impact on the business infrastructure serving the local area. Depopulation reduces the number of potential customers; population growth increases it. In addition, some research suggests that the presence of a well developed retail and service structure may, in itself, generate additional population gain. Prolonged population decline also induces widespread resistance to any effort to reduce the number of functions, and a management style emphasizing risk avoidance and conservation of capital. In contrast, growing areas enjoy access to an expanding array of goods and services, though there is some resistance to unbridled expansion and its possible consequences.

However, population is not the only element affecting the local business structure. Other important factors include the more sophisticated consumer demands of rural residents and their increased mobility. Transportation improvements allow nonmetropolitan residents to travel farther to fewer, high-volume establishments to obtain the variety and quality of goods they have come to expect. And many small establishments that traditionally supplied the needs of the nonmetropolitan population are hard pressed to remain in business. Because most large-scale enterprises locate in the larger population centers, the retail districts of many smaller centers have declined.

Although the research discussed in this chapter suggests a strong association between population shifts and changes in the business infrastructure, the evidence is fragmentary and less than persuasive. In particular, most studies have examined only a few nonmetropolitan places for a brief time. The present study avoids these shortcomings by using comparative cross-sectional data spanning fifty years to examine the impact of population change on business in all nonmetropolitan counties.

Notes

1. Although using population change as the primary independent variable is justified here, there is a sense in which the fact that population change may not be the initial cause is germane. This research delineates how the retail and service structure responds to population change. As long as the impact of causally prior factors is indirect and mediated through population change, no difficulties arise. But, to the extent that antecedent organizational or environmental factors directly affect the business structure of an area, they represent a source of systematic error. By restricting study to those components of the organization most directly affected by population, one can maximize the likelihood that prior causal factors will be mediated by population change.

2. Lord (1982) reports that the incidence of retail shopping outside the county of residence varies significantly from county to county. Outshopping is greatest when a small county is close to a county containing a major retail center. In such instances, the

proportion of all retail purchases made outside the county of residence is often substantial. However, Lord estimates that there have been only modest changes in the proportion of outshopping in the last several decades. This latter point has significant implications for this study. If the proportion of outshopping has not changed significantly over time, it will introduce minimal error into the estimates of the longitudinal impact of population change on rural business presented in later chapters. This fact, coupled with my focus on frequently needed goods and services, minimizes the impact of county permeability.

3. The farm population represented 60 percent of the total county population. The probability of purchase within the county depended on how frequently the goods were needed; 80 percent of the population purchased groceries within the county, while only 42 percent purchased dress clothing there.

4. A detailed definition of the Standard Metropolitan Statistical Area is provided in the *County and City Data Book* (U.S. Bureau of the Census, 1972).

5. To simplify cross-time analysis, I excluded Virginia counties that formerly included independent cities, and a few other counties with unusual histories. The following is a complete list of such counties. Virginia: Albemarle, Alleghany, Augusta, Bedford, Carroll, Frederick, Greensville, Halifax, Henry, Montgomery, Pittsylvania, Rock Bridge, Rockingham, Southampton, Spotsylvania, Wise; Wisconsin: Menominee, Schawano; New Hampshire: Cheshire; Arkansas: Benton, Washington.

2
Historical Population Trends in the Rural United States

To understand the impact of population change on the business infrastructure, we must examine it in an appropriate demographic context. The recent excitement over the rural population turnaround underscores the fact that during most of this century rural areas have experienced widespread outmigration and population decline.

Historical Nonmetropolitan Demographic Trends

Between 1920 and 1970, the rural areas, which had historically dominated the nation, declined in comparison to the rapidly expanding metropolitan sector. In fact, the 1920 census was the first in which the urban population of the nation exceeded the rural. Between 1920 and 1970, the nonmetropolitan United States grew a modest 19.5 percent. The nation as a whole grew by 92 percent, from 106 million in 1920 to 203 million in 1970. Most of the gain came in metropolitan areas, which grew 140 percent during the fifty-year period. Thus, the nonmetropolitan population, while increasing slightly in absolute numbers, declined from 42 to 26 percent of the total population.

The pattern of change within the nonmetropolitan United States has been complex. Although slightly over half of all

15

TABLE 2.1
Summary Measures of Population and Migration Change in Nonmetropolitan
America 1920 to 1970

	1920–1930	1930–1940[a]	1940–1950[a]	1950–1960	1960–1970
Population at Beginning of the decade (000's)	44,633	46,495	48,736	49,581	51,021
Total Population Change (000's)	1,862	2,241	845	1,440	2,153
Total Percentage Change in Population	4.2	4.8	1.7	2.9	4.2
Percentage of Counties Gaining Population	53	64	41	40	47
Total Net Migration (000's)	na	–2,391	–5,437	–6,198	–2,934
Total Net Migration Change (Percentage)	na	–5.1	–11.2	–11.5	–5.8
Percentage of Counties with Inmigration	na	24	12	12	25

[a]Migration figures for 1930–1940 and 1940–1950 are for persons ten years of age
and older at the end of the period

counties experienced a net loss of population during the fifty-year period, relatively few exhibited consistent patterns of either growth or decline. Those that did experienced much more substantial shifts than other counties. Although patterns of mixed growth and decline were common, over 40 percent of all nonmetropolitan counties reached their maximum size by 1930. Counties that peaked early typically suffered the greatest losses by the end of the period. By the same token, counties that peaked late, and particularly those with consistent increase, grew significantly during the period.

The ebbs and flows of change sweeping nonmetropolitan areas between 1920 and 1970 are evident in a decade by decade summary of the period (Table 2.1). The first decade (1920–1930) was one of contrasts. Roughly half the counties suffered a net loss of population, and another 28 percent grew slowly. Yet almost 16 percent of the counties grew more than 2 percent per year, a larger proportion of fast growers than in any other decade (Johnson, 1980:83). This contrast emphasizes the unsettled character of the nonmetropolitan scene during the 1920s. Though the farm population had peaked only a few years earlier, the twenties saw the first widespread introduction of modern agricultural technology in many parts of the country. There was also an economic boom in the nation's industrial base. These two trends accelerated the movement of labor to the nation's urban centers. However, the impact of these factors varied widely across nonmetropolitan areas, and this unevenness, coupled with high rural fertility, resulted in rapid population increase in some areas in contrast to the general trend.

During the Great Depression, rural population increase was greater and more widespread than in the prosperous twenties and forties. This population gain was a function of smaller migration losses, and occurred in spite of the fertility decline caused by the difficult economic times. Families are less likely to move to urban areas when the prospects of economic security are not promising; migration losses in the 1930s were less than half those of the 1940s or 1950s, and were almost certainly lower than those of the 1920s as well. In some areas (e.g., Appalachia) a return stream of migration from metropolitan areas further reduced migration losses. In general, nonmetropolitan counties experienced greater population gains and less net outmigration during the 1930s than at any time up to the turnaround of the 1970s.

The 1940s and 1950s represent the peak of the mass rural-to-urban exodus of the midcentury. The drain of people from rural areas during these decades is evident in the aggregate migration loss of 11.6 million during the twenty-year period. Though these migration losses were partly offset by the substantial natural increase of the baby boom that began in 1947 and continued well into the 1960s, nonmetropolitan growth rates in the 1940s and 1950s were the lowest of this century. Factors underlying this migration include the widespread acceptance of modern agricultural technology in most rural areas and an economic boom that rapidly increased the metropolitan demand for labor during and after World War II.

During the 1960s, fewer counties, though still more than 50 percent, lost population. The number of counties experiencing substantial losses also fell. Prolonged outmigration had sharply reduced the number of mobile people remaining in many nonmetropolitan counties, and by 1960 most local populations had adjusted to the fundamental agricultural and economic forces that underlay the rural-to-urban migration streams of the first half of the twentieth century. In retrospect, it is also likely that the moderating trends of the 1960s represent the first stage of what would eventually become the nonmetropolitan population turnaround (Beale, 1975; Beale and Fuguitt, 1976).

Extent and Duration of Population
Change in County Groups

The brief overview above does not adequately convey the complexity of nonmetropolitan demographic trends. In order to examine the impact of such population shifts in historical context, I have placed each county in a group based on its history of consistent population change in the four decades before 1970. For example, the 478 counties in the group labeled LOSS3070 lost population during each decade from 1930 to 1970 (Table 2.2). Counties in GAIN5070 grew consistently from 1950 to 1970 after losing inhabitants in the 1940s. This classification scheme will be used throughout the analysis as an integrating device to examine the impact population change has on business activity among a diverse group of nonmetropolitan counties.

The various county groups form three distinct clusters. At one extreme, population losses were greatest among counties that declined throughout the period (LOSS3070). These 478 counties sustained by 1970 a net loss of population equivalent to 35 percent of their 1920 population. A somewhat smaller, though still substantial, net loss accrued to counties that began to lose population consistently in 1940. By 1970 the median population for counties in each of these groups was signif-

TABLE 2.2
Population 1970 and Population Change Between 1920 and 1970 by County Group

	1970			1920 to 1970	
	Number	Population	Median Size	Population Change	Percent Change
LOSS3070	478	4,936,725	7,955	-2,641,072	-34.9
LOSS4070	373	5,181,485	11,722	-1,276,415	-19.8
LOSS5070	164	3,393,306	15,812	231,319	7.3
LOSS6070	273	5,939,267	15,774	1,413,318	31.2
GAIN6070	441	7,528,295	14,002	5,342	.1
GAIN5070	142	2,689,389	15,815	522,753	24.1
GAIN4070	80	2,380,144	24,267	734,893	44.7
GAIN3070	474	21,125,493	36,950	9,701,486	84.9
ALL NONMET.	2425	53,174,104	14,889	8,691,624	19.5

icantly smaller than that for any other group. These two groups, and particularly LOSS3070, provide valuable insights into how the county business infrastructure responds to prolonged population decline.

County groups with shorter periods of sustained decline (LOSS5070, LOSS6070) actually gained population during the fifty-year period, as did those with short periods of sustained population increase (GAIN5070, GAIN6070). Except for LOSS6070, the median population size remained relatively stable among these four intermediate groups throughout the study period. In fact, their median sizes were more homogeneous in 1970 than they had been in 1920. By 1970, counties in these groups stood intermediate in size between the county groups subjected to protracted decline and those with prolonged growth. Because most sustained neither substantial nor protracted change, these counties provide a valuable

TABLE 2.3
Median Percentage Change in Population in Each County Group by Decade

	CHANGE 1920-1930	CHANGE 1930-1940	CHANGE 1940-1950	CHANGE 1950-1960	CHANGE 1960-1970
LOSS3070	-1.3	-7.1	-11.9	-12.0	-10.6
LOSS4070	-2.6	6.3	-9.4	-11.4	-6.8
LOSS5070	8.1	5.5	4.4	-8.2	-7.6
LOSS6070	3.9	3.6	3.1	6.6	-5.5
GAIN6070	-1.9	5.2	-5.5	-7.2	5.3
GAIN5070	-1.0	4.2	-4.5	6.6	8.1
GAIN4070	10.4	-4.1	8.8	7.2	9.0
GAIN3070	5.1	8.8	10.6	11.3	11.8
ALL NONMET.	.7	3.6	-2.6	-3.3	-.7

baseline for comparison with counties subjected to more pronounced population shifts.

Among counties with protracted population growth, substantial population gains accrued during the fifty-year period. In fact, GAIN3070 gained population at a rate only slightly lower than that for the nation as a whole. By 1970, the 474 counties in this group contained almost 40 percent of the entire nonmetropolitan population, and were nearly twice as populous as counties in most other nonmetropolitan groups. It is among such counties that the impact of population increase on rural business will be most clearly reflected.

Data on the median percentage change in county size (Table 2.3) provide additional information on population change in the nonmetropolitan United States. The two groups that experienced protracted decline conform quite closely to the overall pattern of change for all nonmetropolitan counties. That is, loss was heaviest in the forties and fifties, with a slackening of the pace in the sixties. The anomalous behavior of LOSS6070 and GAIN6070 becomes clearer in the context of these data. For example, a majority of the counties in LOSS6070 gained population in each decade before 1960; thus the group exhibits many of the properties of a growing rather than a declining group. By the same token, in three of the four decades preceding the sixties, counties in GAIN6070 had been more likely to decline than to grow. This mixed history explains the group's tendencies toward loss rather than growth behavior.

The most striking feature of the two protracted-growth groups (GAIN3070, GAIN4070) is their pattern of population change during the forties and fifties. During these two decades, when most nonmetropolitan counties experienced severe population losses, counties in these groups not only grew, but grew substantially.

In fact, whenever the rate of growth slowed in the nonmetropolitan United States as a whole, as it did from the thirties to the forties, it increased in continuous growth counties (GAIN3070). In this regard at least, continuous-growth counties behaved more like metropolitan than nonmetropolitan counties.

In sum, a complex pattern of population change characterizes the nonmetropolitan United States between 1920 and 1970. Most counties gained population during some part of the period, but population decline was the dominant trend, particularly during the 1940s and 1950s. There is also a strong relationship between the extent and the duration of population change.

The Role of Migration

Historically, most nonmetropolitan areas have lost population to urban centers through migration. Temporal variations in the rate of rural population change have always been primarily a function of such migration, which has varied more over time than has the rate of natural increase. With a few recent exceptions, rural birth rates have always been more than adequate to offset deaths and provide for significant natural increase. Substantial population decline has historically been a function of heavy outmigration. When outmigration has been modest, natural increase has typically sufficed to minimize population losses or allow for modest gains. And until very recently, net inmigration to a nonmetropolitan county virtually guaranteed substantial population gain.

Data on nonmetropolitan migration patterns are not readily available for much of the period studied here. The Census Bureau does provide migration data for the 1950s and 1960s. Before that, net migration must be estimated, because the census contains no migration data for entire decades. The net migration estimates for the 1930s and 1940s were prepared by Gardner and Cohen (1971), who used the forward census survival rate method developed by Hamilton and Henderson (1944). This method can be applied only to cohorts alive at the beginning of the interval;[1] it provides no data for persons less than 10 years of age at the end of the decade. Although Gardner and Cohen sought to estimate migration for this group by other means, the results were not satisfactory. Therefore, for the 1930s and 1940s, I discuss only the migration patterns of those already alive at the beginning of each decade.[2]

Among counties that remained nonmetropolitan in 1974, migration flows were generally smaller in the 1930s than in any other decade (Table 2.4). Nonetheless, the overall pattern of population change for the decade still depended heavily on the magnitude and direction of the migration stream. Migration losses were greatest in the two groups in which all counties lost population (LOSS3070, GAIN4070). In such counties the lower natural increase resulting from the lower fertility levels of the Great Depression did not offset heavy migration losses, although virtually all counties in these groups did experience some natural increase. In contrast, in the two country groups (GAIN3070, LOSS4070) with universal population increase during the 1930s, inmigration was much more common. Except in the continuous growth cohort (GAIN3070), net outmigration was still the rule. Although the number of counties with inmigration was relatively high during the 1930s, most population gains occurred through the traditional pattern of natural increase outpacing migration loss.

TABLE 2.4
**Median Percentage Net Migration and Percentage of Counties with Inmigration
by County Group by Decade, 1930-1970**

	1930 - 1940		1940 - 1950		1950 - 1960		1960 - 1970	
	Net Mig.[a]	% with Inmig.	Net Mig.[a]	% with Inmig.	Net Mig.	% with Inmig.	Net Mig.	% with Inmig.
LOSS3070	-16.2	0.0	-21.4	0.0	-24.1	0.0	-15.4	1.6
LOSS4070	-5.1	18.8	-21.7	0.0	-25.2	0.0	-14.9	1.1
LOSS5070	-6.3	22.0	-11.1	11.0	-25.6	0.0	-16.9	0.0
LOSS6070	-5.2	27.9	-10.1	16.5	-9.0	18.0	-16.2	0.4
GAIN6070	-6.3	21.5	-17.7	4.3	-20.2	0.0	.2	52.4
GAIN5070	-4.6	26.8	-16.0	.7	-7.2	25.3	3.1	42.3
GAIN4070	-12.0	2.5	-2.9	33.8	-7.1	27.6	-1.5	46.3
GAIN3070	.8	54.9	-2.8	39.0	-3.9	37.2	.7	54.6
ALL NONMET.	-6.1	23.8	-14.8	12.2	-16.9	11.7	-8.8	24.7

[a]Estimated median net migration for those ten years of age and over at the end
of the decade

Note: Net Mig. is the median net migration in the county group during the decade

Data presented elsewhere (Johnson, 1981) emphasize the prominent role black migration played in nonmetropolitan population trends of the period. The exodus of blacks from rural areas, which began early in this century, continued during the 1930s despite the lack of economic opportunities in the cities. Although blacks constituted only 12.6 percent of the nonmetropolitan population in 1930, they accounted for 22 percent of the net migration loss between 1930 and 1940. As a result, in the rural black population, declines were greater or gains were smaller than in the rural white population.

The staggering outmigration of the 1940s caused widespread nonmetropolitan population losses. Fueled by World War II and the postwar urban economic boom, the median net migration loss from a nonmetropolitan county in the 1940s was −14.8 percent, more than double what it had been during the 1930s. Only the rising level of natural increase kept the population losses from being greater.

Among the several county groups with widespread population losses during the 1940s (LOSS3070, LOSS4070, GAIN5070), two had median migration losses of more than 21 percent, and there was not a single instance of net inmigration. Even with significant natural increase, counties in these groups still suffered population losses of 10 percent or more. Most other county groups also experienced migration losses. Substantial population gains were evident only in county groups that experienced modest outmigration or net inmigration (GAIN3070, GAIN4070).

As in the 1930s, outmigration was even greater among blacks than among whites (Johnson, 1981). In declining counties with a significant black population, black outmigration often exceeded 25 percent during the 1940s. And black migration losses of 10 percent were common even among counties with a growng black population. In 10 percent of the declining counties, the exodus of blacks was so great that the total population declined despite a growing white population. In all, blacks accounted for 24 percent of the decade's net outmigration from rural areas, although in 1940 they had represented only 12.2 percent of the nonmetropolitan population.

The rural population drain peaked during the 1950s, when nonmetropolitan counties lost nearly 6.2 million people in exchanges with metropolitan areas. This figure represents a loss of 12.5 percent of the entire nonmetropolitan population alive in 1950. Because of the baby boom, the nonmetropolitan population actually grew slightly more during the 1950s than it had during the 1940s. But migration losses were substantially higher.

Outmigration was heaviest from the three groups of counties that had begun to lose population consistently by 1950 and in GAIN6070. In each of these cohorts, the median loss from outmigration was more than 20 percent. Not a single county among the 1491 in these groups had inmigration. In contrast, counties that gained population during the 1950s were able to do so because they experienced modest migration losses, or in some instances, enjoyed inmigration. Among county groups with population gain in the 1950s, the median rate of outmigration never exceeded 10 percent, and a significant number of countries had net inmigration. However, even among counties that gained population, net outmigration prevailed. Although growing counties generally had greater natural increase than declining ones, the differential was much less significant than for migration. This substantial difference between the rate of net outmigration in growing and declining counties was the primary cause of the differential pattern of population change in the 1950s.

During the 1960s net outmigration moderated significantly; the median loss fell to 9 percent (from 17 percent in the 1950s), and net inmigration became common among counties with histories of population increase. Inmigration remained rare in historical decline counties, although median net out-flows of population did subside in most declining counties— more, in fact, than they did in growing ones. The net outflow of population from nonmetropolitan areas dropped by 53 percent to only 2.9 million in the 1960s, foreshadowing the general trend of the 1970s, although no one perceived this at the time. However, the overall nonmetropolitan population gain during the 1960s was only slightly higher than it had been during the 1950s, because of the slowdown in natural increase that marked the end of the postwar baby boom.

The Pattern of Natural Increase

Data on natural increase during the 1930s and 1940s at the county level are not readily available. Between 1950 and 1970, however, basic changes occurred in the rate of natural increase.

During the fifties all nonmetropolitan areas had high rates of natural increase; even among counties with forty years of decline the median rate of natural increase exceeded 10 percent (Table 2.5). These substantial natural gains dampened or reversed the effect of the decade's enormous rural-to-urban exodus.

TABLE 2.5
Median Percentage Natural Increase and Percentage of Counties with Natural Decrease
by County Group, 1950 - 1970

	1950 - 1960		1960 - 1965		1965 - 1970	
	Median Natural Increase	% with Natural Decrease	Median Natural Increase	% with Natural Decrease	Median Natural Increase	% with Natural Decrease
LOSS3070	11.8	0.0	3.6	8.8	1.1	32.1
LOSS4070	14.0	0.0	4.9	0.8	3.0	11.8
LOSS5070	16.7	0.0	5.8	0.0	3.8	3.7
LOSS6070	18.8	0.0	6.4	0.0	4.0	3.7
GAIN6070	11.5	0.2	4.5	2.7	2.6	12.2
GAIN5070	14.9	0.7	6.3	0.7	3.8	6.3
GAIN4070	16.5	0.0	6.5	1.3	3.8	3.8
GAIN3070	16.4	0.0	6.3	0.2	4.3	1.9
ALL NONMET	14.3	0.1	5.3	2.4	3.2	11.9

Between 1960 and 1965 the rate of natural increase slowed down substantially. Over these five years, the median increase for each county group was markedly less than half of what it had been over the preceding ten. The slowdown was relatively consistent across all groups, with long-term losers slowing at only a slightly faster rate than long-term gainers. Also, more counties experienced natural decrease. During the 1950s, natural decline was rare, but during the early 1960s it occurred in 8.8 percent of the counties with protracted population decline.

Clearly these data are not in themselves sufficient to suggest an end to the traditional pattern of large natural increase and heavy outmigration from nonmetropolitan areas. Conclusive evidence of a basic change in rural patterns of natural increase is, however, apparent in the data for 1965–1970. During this period the pace of natural increase continued to slow compared both to the record pace of the 1950s, and to the slower rates of the early 1960s. Reductions were pronounced among counties in the protracted-decline groups but were evident even among counties with long-term population increase. Natural decline also became more widespread.

The trend in natural increase reflects in large part the secular decline of fertility that marked the end of the baby boom. In some areas natural increase was also hindered by an age structure distorted by long years of age-selective outmigration. With fertility levels steadily declining in the 1960s, migration became a more prominent source of population increase. The impact of such inmigration is quite evident in the data for the 1970s, reviewed in Chapter 5.

The natural decrease that became increasingly common in the 1960s is unusual in the U.S. experience. It did occur for a time during the Great Depression as a result of extremely low fertility (Dorn, 1936), but it was short-lived, disappearing with the onset of World War II. Isolated instances of decline appeared again in the 1950s but were also typically short-lived (Beale, 1969). Natural decrease first became widespread between 1965 and 1970, when it affected 12 percent of all nonmetropolitan counties. In the early 1970s, this figure reached 15 percent (Johnson and Purdy, 1980).

Several studies suggest that a principal cause of natural decrease is a distorted age structure caused by long-sustained migration of young adults from the area (Beale, 1969; Chang, 1974; Markides and Tracy, 1977). In counties with such a distorted age structure, the depleted ranks of young adults do not produce enough children to offset the deaths of older residents. This problem is particularly acute when secular trends tend toward lower birth rates. A secondary cause of natural decrease may be that women in such areas are having fewer children than their counterparts in growing areas; however, even in declining areas the fertility rates remain well above the replacement level (Chang, 1974; Markides and Tracy, 1977).

Migration, Natural Increase, and the Age Structure

Data on changes in the age structure between 1950 and 1970 demonstrate the distorting effect of migration and help

TABLE 2.6
Median Age, Median Percentage of the Population Under Age 5 or Greater than 64
in 1970, and Percentage Change 1950 to 1970 by County Group

	Median Age		Under Age 5		Greater than 64	
	Median 1970	Change 1950-1970	Median 1970	Change 1950-1970	Median 1970	Change 1950-1970
LOSS3070	34.5	4.6	7.1	-34.3	15.8	58.5
LOSS4070	31.5	4.1	7.9	-32.2	13.6	59.6
LOSS5070	29.8	4.3	8.0	-36.8	11.6	68.9
LOSS6070	29.3	0.8	8.2	-30.5	11.3	36.5
GAIN6070	30.6	3.0	7.9	-29.8	12.9	46.3
GAIN5070	28.1	-0.9	8.5	-22.5	10.9	17.1
GAIN4070	27.7	-1.1	8.4	-25.8	10.5	20.4
GAIN3070	27.9	-1.4	8.5	-24.4	10.2	17.5
ALL NONMET.	30.1	2.2	8.0	-29.9	12.3	44.6

explain the rising incidence of natural decrease. They also help show how population change influences nonmetropolitan business trends, because the age structure of the population influences consumer buying habits.

In 1950, all county groups had roughly similar age structures, but during the next twenty years significant demographic changes occurred. The initially high rates of both natural increase and net outmigration began moderating in the sixties. Because migration is age selective and fertility declined, over the period as a whole the oldest segment of the population increased while the youngest decreased.

By 1970, a pattern emerged linking the duration of population change to the median percentage of the population in given age categories (Table 2.6). In 1950, the proportion of the population under 5 exceeded that over 64 in each county group (Johnson, 1980). By 1970, the pattern was completely reversed. The proportionate decline in youngsters was a function of the temporal decline in fertility, exacerbated in the protracted-decline groups by years of outmigration among young adults. The proportion of persons over 64 increased by roughly 20 percent among counties with several decades of population increase, but by 60 percent or more in counties with protracted decline. This combination of fertility declines and large concentrations of older adults in protracted-decline groups made them much more prone to natural decrease in the late 1960s.

The median age in all nonmetropolitan counties increased by 2.2 years between 1950 and 1970. Median age rose significantly in counties that had begun losing population consistently by 1950, and fell in counties that had begun growing consistently before 1950. While the population in declining counties was aging, that in growing counties was becoming younger.

The Geographic Distribution of
Growing and Declining Counties

Researchers have long recognized the regional variations in demographic trends in the nonmetropolitan United States (Zelinsky, 1962; Lee et al., 1957; Eldridge and Thomas, 1964; Beale, 1964). To understand the demographic context surrounding rural business change, we therefore need information about the geographic character of nonmetropolitan population trends.

A majority or near majority of the nonmetropolitan counties in several of the subregions devised by Beale and Fuguitt (1975)[3] had suffered steady population decline for at least twenty years by 1970 (Table 2.7). Such protracted decline was common in the Great Plains, Southern Corn Belt, Southern Appalachian Coal Fields, Mississippi Delta, Coastal Plain Tobacco and Peanut Belt, and Old Coastal Plain Cotton Belt (Figure 2.1). Except for Southern Appalachia, these areas have long been predominantly agricultural, and they suffered heavy outmigration as capital replaced labor on the farm.

Such agricultural changes affected the grain-producing areas of the Midwest first; many rural counties of the Great Plains reached their maximum population early in this century and

TABLE 2.7
Population Change in Subregions of the United States

Subregion Code	Subregion Name	Extended Loss	Recent Loss	Recent Growth	Extended Growth	Number of Counties
1	Northern New England	5.6%	19.5	36.1	38.8	36
2	Northeastern Metro Belt	4.5%	2.3	9.0	84.2	44
3	Mohawk Valley New York, Penn. Border	9.1%	9.1	18.2	63.7	33
4	Northern Appalachian Coal Fields	29.1%	25.5	21.8	23.6	55
5	Lower Great Lakes Industrial	0 %	2.5	3.8	93.7	79
6	Upper Great Lakes	22.8%	12.9	30.0	34.3	70
7	Dairy Belt	25.5%	6.4	42.6	25.5	47
8	Central Corn Belt	39.8%	29.2	13.5	17.4	178
9	Southern Corn Belt	65.9%	7.6	21.3	5.3	132
10	Southern Interior Uplands	27.1%	6.1	48.0	19.0	148
11	Southern Appalachian Coal Fields	49.4%	33.4	16.0	1.3	75
12	Blue Ridge, Great Smokies, Great Valley	24.4%	9.5	40.5	25.7	74
13	Southern Piedmont	30.5%	9.6	23.8	36.2	105
14	Coastal Plain Tobacco and Peanut Belt	12.7%	49.2	12.7	25.4	63
15	Old Coastal Plain Cotton Belt	57.0%	11.7	24.0	7.2	179
16	Mississippi Delta	61.6%	23.1	13.4	1.9	52
17	Gulf and South Atlantic Coast	1.5%	21.2	31.8	45.5	66
18	Florida Peninsula	0 %	5.3	10.5	84.2	19
19	East Texas and Adj. Coastal Plain	46.1%	4.8	42.3	6.8	104
20	Ozark - Ouchita Uplands	16.9%	2.4	79.5	1.2	83
21	Rio Grande	36.6%	30.7	14.4	18.2	104
22	Southern Great Plains	48.4%	29.2	12.0	10.4	192
23	Northern Great Plains	58.7%	24.4	9.0	7.8	254
24	Rocky Mts., Mormon Valleys, Columbia Basin	20.7%	27.6	24.9	26.9	145
25	Northern Pacific Coast	0 %	15.6	25.0	59.4	32
26	Southwest	0 %	7.2	34.0	58.9	56
Total		35.1% (851)	18.1 (437)	24.1 (583)	19.6 (554)	2425

have declined since. Later, as agricultural innovations spread to crops produced in the South, this area also was subjected to heavy outmigration and widespread population decline. Black outmigration generally exceeded that for whites. For example, between 1940 and 1950 the black nonmetropolitan population declined by 6 percent because 22 percent of the black nonmetropolitan population alive in 1930 were lost to net outmigration. The white population grew by 3 percent

31

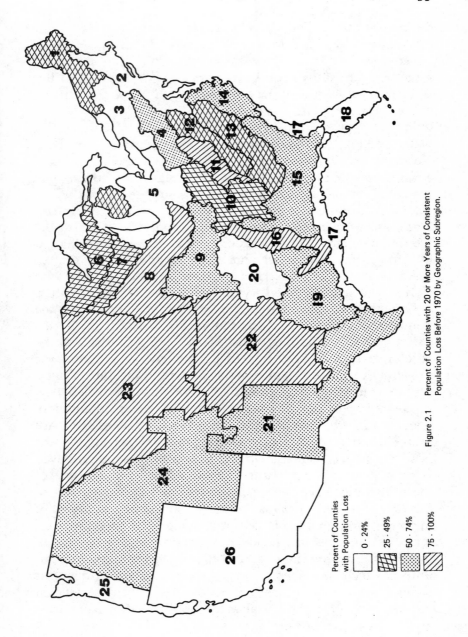

Figure 2.1   Percent of Counties with 20 or More Years of Consistent
Population Loss Before 1970 by Geographic Subregion.

Percent of Counties
with Population Loss

0 - 24%
25 - 49%
50 - 74%
75 - 100%

during the same period, with natural increase more than offsetting a migration loss of 10 percent (Johnson, 1981). In general, population shifts in these subregions were primarily a function of the westward movement of population and the shift from rural areas of the Midwest and South to the nation's metropolitan centers.

In several other subregions where a majority of the counties were declining by 1970, including the Central Corn Belt, Northern Appalachian Coal Fields, Rio Grande, and East Texas subregions, the decline did not begin until the 1950s. Many of the same factors influencing subregions with protracted histories of loss were at work here, although in these areas, except in the Central Corn Belt and some parts of the Rio Grande, agricultural productivity has always been limited by topography and water shortages. In addition, several of these areas have large concentrations of poor people who clung to the land despite very limited economic opportunities.

Growth predominated in the Far West, Florida, and the nonmetropolitan areas adjacent to the Midwestern and Northeastern urban-industrial belts. Many rural counties in the latter two regions have benefited for some time from their proximity to major urban centers, as decentralization of metropolitan industry and suburbanization have provided new residents for surrounding nonmetropolitan areas. In addition, many nonmetropolitan counties in these subregioins also have a significant base of manufacturing plants that supply the nearby industrial centers. Florida, of course, has long received large streams of inmigrants from the North, and many of these migrants have settled in the nonmetropolitan parts of the state. The West has also attracted substantial numbers of migrants throughout this century, though the preferred terminus within this vast region has certainly changed through the years. Initially, the migrants converged on Southern California, which continued to receive large numbers of migrants throughout the study period. Later, there were significant inflows of migrants to rural areas of the Pacific Northwest and to New Mexico and Arizona.

In recent years attention has focused on several subregions where widespread growth has followed decades of population decline. This turnaround is largely a phenomenon of the 1970s and, therefore, beyond the purview of this chapter, but the first instances of it were already evident in some subregions during the late 1960s. The best example is in the Ozark-Ouachita Uplands, where just under 80 percent of the non-metropolitan counties began to grow after decades of decline. Other areas of the South with prominent recent growth include the Southern Interior Uplands and the Blue Ridge–Great Smokies. In the Midwest, many counties in the Dairy Belt and Upper Great Lakes regions were also experiencing population gains by the 1960s after long histories of decline. Although the factors underlying this remarkable turnaround are complex, the myriad recreational opportunities in such areas are known to have spurred population growth through inmigration, particularly of retired workers (Beale, 1975; Beale and Fuguitt, 1975). The first stirrings of the population turnaround were also evident in the Gulf and South Atlantic Coast, East Texas, and the Southern Piedmont, where recent industrial development has helped attract and retain population.

Characteristics of Growing and Declining Counties

The factors underlying the growth of some nonmetropolitan areas and the decline of others during the first seven decades of this century have been examined in detail elsewhere (Lee et al., 1957; Beale, 1975; Zelinsky, 1962). I do not intend to expand on that work. Rather, I focus here on several county characteristics that are relevant to how population change influences rural business.

Population Change and Urban Centers

Past research suggests that, at least before the nonmetropolitan population turnaround, large urban places were more likely to grow than small ones (Northam, 1969; Hassinger, 1975b; Fuguitt and Deeley, 1966; Fuguitt, 1965b; Tarver and Beale, 1968). The statements in the following section apply only to the period before 1970; as Chapter 5 shows, many of the historical relationships between urban size and adjacency no longer hold during the turnaround. Larger urban places provide a wider range of goods, services, and employment opportunities that enhance the competitive position of their surrounding areas and draw population to them.

Data for 1970 reveal that counties with long histories of population gain were much more likely to contain a large urban place than were other counties (Table 2.8). In general, a moderately strong positive association exists between a county's prior pattern of population change and the size of the largest place in the county in 1970. Overall, 53 percent of extended-growth counties, but only 4 percent of protracted-decline counties, contained an urban place of at least 10,000 in 1970. Because data on size of largest place are available here only for 1970, it is difficult to demonstrate a causal relationship between size of place and county growth. However, there is strong evidence that a similar relationship between size of largest place and future population change existed in 1930 (Johnson, 1980).

Future population growth was also more common among counties with larger percentages of urban population in 1930 (Table 2.9). Counties with extended population gain were most likely to have had large concentrations of urban residents in 1930. In contrast, over two-thirds of the counties that experienced protracted decline between 1930 and 1970 had been totally rural in 1930. Their very rural character in part explains their subsequent population losses. Such counties depended heavily on agriculture, which was rapidly changing from labor intensive to capital intensive during the middle of the century. As they lacked significant towns to attract alternative employment or growth opportunities, they were subject to heavy outmigration.

Between 1930 and 1970 the U.S. population concentrated increasingly in urban places. This trend occurred in nonmetropolitan parts of the country as well as in metropolitan areas. In 1930, only 29 percent of the nonmetropolitan counties had over 25 percent of their population residing in urban places. By 1970, the figure had increased to over 55 percent.

TABLE 2.8
Historical Pattern of Growth or Decline by Size of Largest Place, 1970

| | | Pattern of Population Change | | | |
		Extended Decline	Recent Decline	Recent Growth	Extended Growth
	Less than 2,500	55%	27%	36%	9%
Size of	2,500 to 9,999	41	48	50	38
Largest					
Place	10,000 to 24,999	4	19	13	34
	More than 24,999	0	5	1	19
		100%	99%	100%	100%
		(851)	(437)	(583)	(554)
	Missing = 0		Gamma = .52		

Note: Extended Decline includes LOSS3070 and LOSS4070
Recent Decline includes LOSS5070 and LOSS6070
Recent Growth includes GAIN5070 and GAIN6070
Extended Growth includes GAIN4070 and GAIN3070

TABLE 2.9
Percentage of the Population That Was Urban in 1930 by
Subsequent Pattern of Population Change

| | | Pattern of Population Change | | | |
		Extended Decline	Recent Decline	Recent Growth	Extended Growth
	No Urban Residents	67%	49%	60%	27%
Percent	1% to 25%	19	16	21	17
Urban					
1930	25% to 50%	12	25	16	38
	More than 50%	2	10	3	18
		100%	100%	100%	100%
		(851)	(437)	(582)	(554)
	Missing Case = 0		Gamma = .38		

Note: Extended Decline includes LOSS3070 and LOSS4070
Recent Decline includes LOSS5070 and LOSS6070
Recent Growth includes GAIN5070 and GAIN6070
Extended Growth includes GAIN4070 and GAIN3070

TABLE 2.10
Percentage of the Population That Was Urban in 1970 by Historical Pattern
of Population Change

| | | Pattern of Population Change | | | |
		Extended Decline	Recent Decline	Recent Growth	Extended Growth
	No Urban Residents	54%	28%	35%	10%
Percent Urban 1970	1% to 25%	9	11	13	11
	25% to 50%	27	33	37	41
	More than 50%	10	28	15	38
		100% (851)	100% (437)	100% (583)	100% (554)

Missing Case = 0   Gamma = .37

Note: Extended Decline includes LOSS3070 and LOSS4070
        Recent Decline includes LOSS5070 and LOSS6070
        Recent Growth includes GAIN5070 and GAIN6070
        Extended Growth includes GAIN4070 and GAIN3070

TABLE 2.11
Metropolitan Adjacency in 1970 by Historical Pattern of Population Change

| | | Pattern of Population Change | | | |
		Extended Decline	Recent Decline	Recent Growth	Extended Growth
Metropolitan Adjacency, 1970	Not Adjacent	71%	67%	58%	43%
	Adjacent	29	23	42	57
		100% (851)	100% (437)	100% (583)	100% (554)

Missing Case = 0   Gamma = .32

Note: Extended Decline includes LOSS3070 and LOSS4070
        Recent Decline includes LOSS5070 and LOSS6070
        Recent Growth includes GAIN5070 and GAIN6070
        Extended Growth includes GAIN4070 and GAIN3070

Extended-growth counties still tended to be the most urban in 1970, with over 79 percent of the group having at least 25 percent of their residents in urban places (Table 2.10). Counties with prolonged decline remained the least urban; in fact, a majority of this group were still entirely rural. A significant proportion of the recent-growth counties also had little or no urban population. In retrospect, this deviation from the general trend in the data represents the leading edge of the nonmetropolitan population turnaround.

A county's history of population growth or decline is also influenced by its proximity to a metropolitan area. Counties with histories of population increase are much more likely to be adjacent to a metropolitan area than are those that have declined (Table 2.11). By 1970, over 60 percent of the nonadjacent counties were declining, but only 40 percent of the adjacent counties (Johnson, 1980). Since 1970, the number of growing nonadjacent counties has accelerated, reflecting the nonmetropolitan turnaround (Beale, 1975; Beale and Fuguitt, 1976; Johnson and Purdy, 1980).

Many researchers have documented the fact that in recent times nonmetropolitan population growth has been more common in areas near metropolitan centers (Campbell, 1975; Fuguitt, 1965b). In fact, the trend has long been for growth within an urban area to move outward from the core through the city proper, then to the suburbs, and finally beyond (Hawley, 1976). Thus, much of the growth in counties adjacent to metropolitan areas is essentially spillover from the nearby metropolitan area. Or, as Hawley (1976) suggests, the definition of the S.M.S.A. no longer delineates the actual urban unit. Research documents the desire of many citizens to reside outside a metropolitan area, yet close to it (Zuiches and Fuguitt, 1972; Fuguitt and Zuiches, 1975). Some of these individuals may be acting on their desires.

Because metropolitan adjacency and size of largest place affect a county simultaneously, their combined impact must be considered. Counties that have large urban places and are adjacent to metropolitan areas have been particularly prone to growth, whereas nonadjacent counties with no significant urban places have been the most likely candidates for decline.

TABLE 2.12
Median Percentage of the Labor Force Employed in Manufacturing and Agriculture
and Percent Change 1950 to 1970 by County Group

	1950		1970		1950 - 1970	
	Median % in Manuf.	Median % in Agric.	Median % in Manuf.	Median % in Agric.	Percent Change Manuf.	Percent Change Agric.
LOSS3070	3.1	49.2	8.9	25.9	110.8	-44.5
LOSS4070	7.6	48.8	20.0	16.1	135.9	-63.3
LOSS5070	8.0	33.4	16.7	14.9	75.0	-64.8
LOSS6070	7.0	32.8	13.7	14.1	56.3	-50.4
GAIN6070	11.6	39.5	25.6	10.2	98.6	-70.8
GAIN5070	11.1	34.8	19.3	8.9	63.6	-66.4
GAIN4070	12.4	26.6	15.9	10.2	35.0	-56.5
GAIN3070	19.9	21.3	26.3	6.3	27.7	-24.4
ALL NONMET.	9.3	37.6	19.2	12.3	75.0	-61.6

In effect, to have an equal probability of growth a nonadjacent county has needed a substantially larger urban place within its boundaries (Johnson, 1980).

Selected Labor Force Characteristics and Population Change

The composition of the labor force in a nonmetropolitan area affects both its prospects for population growth or decline and its business community. In areas heavily dependent on agriculture, the business infrastructure is sensitive to factors that may be inconsequential in communities oriented to manufacturing.

It has long been recognized that the greatest population losses have occurred in predominantly agricultural nonmetropolitan areas (Beale, 1975; Zelinsky, 1962). Such depopulation stems from the convergence, during the nineteenth century and the first sixty years of the twentieth, of two major historical trends: the replacement of labor by capital in agriculture, and the increased demand for labor in the nation's urban industrial centers.

Table 2.12 shows relationship between population change and the percentage of the labor force employed in agriculture and related extractive industries such as mining and fishing. Between 1950 and 1970, sustained population losses have been more likely in areas with large concentrations of agricultural employees, even though the agricultural labor force had already contracted significantly in most nonmetropolitan counties before 1950 (Johnson, 1981). In each of the protracted-decline groups almost 50 percent of the labor force was still employed in agriculture in 1950. Subsequent population losses in such counties reflect continuing adjustments as the demand for and supply of agricultural workers moved toward equilibrium. The proportion of the work force engaged in agriculture was smaller in county groups with intermittent growth and decline and smallest among counties with histories of protracted population increase.

Between 1950 and 1970 the median percentage of the labor force employed in agriculture decreased markedly in each county group. The decrements were slightly larger among growing counties, and by 1970 no group with a growing populaton had much more than a tenth of its workers engaged in agriculture. The decrease in agricultural employment was slightly less pronounced among counties with histories of population decline. Still, in both of the extended-decline groups over 25 percent of the available jobs shifted from the agricultural to the nonagricultural sector. Despite such massive shifts, counties subjected to continuous population decline remained the most dependent on agricultural jobs in 1970. Many of these counties were destined to continue declining during the 1970s; agricultural counties were among the least likely to participate in the population turnaround (Beale, 1975; Brown and Beale, 1981).

As agricultural employment declined, many nonmetropolitan areas sought to develop other employment opportunities in order to retain and if possible increase local population. Attracting new manufacturing jobs has long been the basic strategy of rural development programs focused on reversing population decline in nonmetropolitan areas (Beale and Fuguitt, 1975). Whether because of such rural development programs or because nonmetropolitan areas have lower land costs, less expensive and more abundant labor, and improved transportation to markets, there has been a significant increase in the number of manufacturing jobs in nonmetropolitan areas during the last several decades. For example, between 1960 and 1970 about 1.25 million manufacturing jobs were added in nonmetropolitan areas. This represented an annual rate of increase of 3.4 percent, well over twice that achieved in metropolitan areas (North Central Regional Center for Rural Development, 1974). Most of these new manufacturing jobs were in the South, and relatively few were in totally rural counties.

Counties with large proportions of manufacturing workers had consistently higher rates of population growth and in-migration between 1950 and 1970 (Beale and Fuguitt, 1975). Within the scheme used here, counties in the two groups that began losing population before 1950 had relatively few manufacturing workers in 1950. Among counties that would soon begin to decline (LOSS5070, LOSS6070), the median percentages of workers engaged in manufacturing were slightly higher, but still below the overall median. Counties that began growing consistently in the 1940s, as well as those that would soon begin to grow, had a higher percentage of workers engaged in manufacturing than did any of the declining groups. The highest median percentage of manufacturing employment in 1950 was in the county group with protracted population growth. There is also evidence that large concentrations of manufacturing employees stimulated population gains in nonmetropolitan areas before 1950. Counties that gained population between 1930 and 1950 had much larger concentrations of manufacturing employees than did counties with steady decline or mixed histories of population change (Johnson, 1981).

The proportion of the labor force engaged in manufacturing increased significantly in each group between 1950 and 1970. The bulk of the gain resulted from the creation of many new manufacturing jobs in nonmetropolitan areas; a smaller part of it was a statistical artifact resulting from the contraction of the agricultural labor force. In fact, by 1970 some of the long-term growth counties had larger industrial bases than many metropolitan centers.

Income and Population Change

Variations in family income among the counties are important in this study for at least three reasons. First, counties with relatively high family incomes are likely to have more complex business infrastructures than poorer counties of similar size and population history. Other things being equal, a wealthier local population will use part of its additional buying power to purchase goods and services a poorer population cannot afford. Second, retailers use income levels to select new markets for expansion. Finally, counties with high income levels are also more likely to retain current residents and attract new ones than counties with lower income levels. Evidence from the nonmetropolitan turnaround suggests that economic factors may not be as strong as they were once believed to be, but incomes are still relevant to this research.

No totally consistent pattern is evident in the income data for 1949, but the two protracted-decline groups had lower medians than the two extended-gain groups (Table 2.13). Among the four intermediate groups, both groups that would soon begin to grow had relatively low income levels in 1949, whereas the two destined to decline had relatively high income levels. Real median family income for all nonmetropolitan areas more than doubled between 1949 and 1969. All groups gained substantially, but gains were greater for the growing than for the declining groups.

The result of these differential rates of change was to make the pattern much more consistent by 1969. With a few minor exceptions, median family income correlates strongly with population change in 1969. Counties with protracted decline had the lowest income levels, the four intermediate-growth groups had intermediate income levels, and the protracted-

TABLE 2.13
Median Family Income Corrected for Inflation and
Percentage Change in Income, 1949 and 1969

	Median Income 1949	Median Income 1969	Percent Change 1949-1969
LOSS3070	2,987	5,767	97
LOSS4070	2,156	5,236	125
LOSS5070	3,223	5,975	87
LOSS6070	3,875	7,160	86
GAIN6070	2,174	5,871	152
GAIN5070	2,921	7,116	129
GAIN4070	3,777	7,639	104
GAIN3070	3,646	7,637	115
ALL NONMET.	3,014	6,351	113

Note: All incomes reported in 1967 dollars

growth groups had the highest incomes. Businesses in pro-tracted-gain counties had not only more but wealthier customers.

Summary

By 1970 slightly more than half of all nonmetropolitan counties were losing population. Relatively few either lost or gained population consistently from 1930 to 1970, but more than a third lost population consistently from 1940 onward. There was little difference in median county population among the groups in 1920. However, by 1970 counties with protracted loss typically were significantly smaller, those with mixed periods of growth and decline remained stable, and those with extended growth were substantially larger. In general, the longer counties consistently grew or declined, the greater the gains or losses. Population decline has been widespread in the agricultural heartland. In contrast, counties in the West and the urban-industrial belts of the Northeast and Middle

West were more likely to grow. Near the end of the period a turnaround from decline to growth was evident in areas of the Midwest and South near recreational attractions and in newly industrialized areas of what has come to be called the sunbelt. This turnaround was the leading edge of the remarkable rural renaissance of the 1970s.

Nonmetropolitan population decline has long been a function of outmigration exceeding local natural increase. Population gains occurred when migration losses were offset by natural increase, or less frequently when a county had net inmigration. Nonmetropolitan population losses peaked during the great rural-to-urban exodus of the 1940s and 1950s and subsided somewhat during the 1960s. By 1970, protracted age-specific outmigration coupled with a declining birth rate occasioned a significant aging of the population in counties with histories of protracted decline. The median age remained relatively stable in counties with population increase, though even they were not spared migration losses of young adults. As a result, the percentage of the population over 64 increased in each county group, while the percentage under 5 declined in each. In 5 percent of the counties, the age structure was so distorted by 1970 that natural decrease was occurring.

Counties with histories of population decline were least likely to have an urban place of significant size within their boundaries and were not likely to be adjacent to a metropolitan area. Growing counties were more likely to include a large town or small city, to have a large urban population, and to be adjacent to a metropolitan area. Thus, the more remote and rural a county was the more likely it was to decline.

Protracted-decline counties still had the heaviest concentrations of agricultural workers in 1970, despite a substantial decline in agricultural employment in all county groups between 1950 and 1970. In contrast, extended-gain counties had the largest proportions of manufacturing workers, even though all county groups gained manufacturing jobs during the period. Real incomes nearly doubled in each county group between 1949 and 1969, but family incomes in declining counties still lagged behind those in growing counties by a significant margin in 1970.

Population shifts of the magnitude and duration summarized above significantly affected the local business infrastructure that developed to serve the needs of nonmetropolitan residents. Chapters 3 and 4 deal with how the rural retail and service sectors, respectively, reacted to these shifts.

Notes

1. The forward census survival method estimates net migration by calculating how many individuals in a given age-sex-race category would be expected to survive through an interval and then comparing the estimate to the actual number of residents alive at the end of the interval. The difference between the expected and observed number of residents is the estimate of net migration for that race-age-sex cohort. To estimate what proportion of a cohort survived the decade, Gardner and Cohen applied the national survival rates to each county. This procedure obviously distorts the estimates, as county mortality rates rarely coincide with those for the nation. However, it was the best method available, because the quality of state mortality and fertility data was very uneven for the 1930s. Gardner and Cohen estimated migration only for whites and blacks. Such a procedure introduces minimal error, because all other races combined represented less than 1 percent of the total nonmetropolitan population.

2. Excluding those under age 10 from the study of migration patterns obviously distorts the analysis somewhat. However, it is unlikely to invalidate either comparisons among the county groups during a given decade or comparisons between decades, because migration patterns for those under age 10 are largely a function of their parents' movements. I am satisfied that Gardner and Cohen's estimates reflect the overall direction and magnitude of county-level migration streams, although they are only estimates and cannot be relied upon to be accurate to the last digit.

3. I gratefully acknowledge Calvin Beale's permission to use the subregions he and Glenn Fuguitt developed. A more detailed discussion of these subregions, with particular reference to the nonmetropolitan population turnaround of the 1970s, is presented in Beale and Fuguitt (1975) and in Brown and Beale (1981).

3
The Historical Impact of Population Change on Rural Retailing

Retailing is generally the most important component of the local business infrastructure in nonmetropolitan counties. Residents obtain many of the necessities of everyday life from nearby retail stores, and most retailers depend on the proximate population for the bulk of their business. This symbiotic relationship makes retailing acutely sensitive to changes in the size of the local population. This chapter provides a detailed assessment of the impact of population change on retailing between 1929 and 1972.

Data and Procedure

Since 1929, the Bureau of the Census has collected data on retail trade in U.S. counties, as part of the Census of Business.[1] Data are available for 1929 and 1939, and at roughly five year intervals from 1948 onward. Data through 1972 are included here under the assumption that there is a slight lag between population change and its reflection in retailing. There have been periodic revisions of the definitions, enumeration procedures, and criteria used by the Census Bureau to collect retail data. Many of these revisions, and their likely impact on comparative cross-sectional analysis, are discussed in detail elsewhere (Johnson, 1980). In general, such revisions make exact historical comparisons impossible, but do not

45

obscure the general trends in the data, nor do they preclude comparisons of population subgroups over time.

To assess change in countywide retail activity, I have examined three variables over time. The first is total volume of retail sales, corrected for inflation. Although not itself a component of the retail structure, sales volume is important because it mediates the relationship between population change and retail organizational structure. A population shift will be reflected most immediately in retail sales. Later, as organizational structure begins to adjust to revenue shifts, other changes in retailing can be expected.

The second dependent variable is change in the number of retail establishments serving a county. Establishments are the most permanent elements of the local retail structure, because the capital expenses involved in opening or closing them make them relatively insensitive to short-term population fluctuations or other changes. Sustained population change, however, is expected to result in the addition or elimination of units.

The final variable is change in the number of retail employees in each county, including partners and proprietors of unincorporated businesses as well as paid employees in both incorporated and unincorporated businesses. Manipulating employment levels is a traditional means of accommodating to short-term fluctuations in demand, because hiring or laying off workers is less expensive than opening or closing new units.[2]

Together the employment and establishment variables make up the retail sector of the local economy. To some extent, they constitute alternative adjustments to demand shifts; however, at best they are only partially interchangeable. Drastic population change requires adjustments in both components.

I have supplemented the data on aggregate retail activity with detailed data on specific types of retailing (e.g., shopping goods, convenience goods, etc.), in order to ascertain whether, as Bollinger (1972) suggests, population change exerts a differential impact on various segments of retailing. The availability of such data, however, varies from census to census, by revisions of the classification schemes used, and by Census Bureau suppressions of data for confidentiality. Because of the uneven pace of inflation during the past half-century, all sales and income data presented in this and the following chapter have been standardized using cost of living data and are expressed in constant 1967 dollars.

The widespread income gains and inflation that affected the nonmetropolitan United States during the period studied represent just two of several factors whose impact on the retail and service sectors was independent of population change. These rival causal factors complicate the task of delineating the impact of population change, but the problem is simplified because many of them affected all counties in roughly the same way. Income gains, Census Bureau revisions, and general economic conditions (except during the Depression) all tended to increase the demand for goods and services in both growing and declining counties. In contrast, population change tended to stimulate demand in growing counties and dampen it in declining ones. Because the direction of retail change was one of gain for both growing and declining counties, to ascertain the impact of population change we must focus on the magnitude of the gains among the two types of counties. For instance, each county group enjoyed a substantial increase in real income during the study period, and one would therefore expect sales increases in each county group. In declining counties population loss partially offset the positive effect of income gains on retail demand. In contrast, among counties where both population and incomes consistently increased, demand accelerated dramatically.

Population Change and Its Impact on Retailing

Between 1929 and 1972, inflation-corrected retail spending in the nonmetropolitan United States increased from 25.7 to 82.8 billion dollars, an increase of 222 percent (Table 3.1). This gain is even more remarkable in view of the very modest rural population increase during the period. Impressive as

TABLE 3.1
Total Retail Sales, Establishments, and Employment 1972 and Percentage Change
in These Components Between 1929 and 1972 by County Group for Nonmetropolitan
and All U.S. Counties.

	Retail Sales		Retail Establishments		Retail Employment	
	Total 1972	Percent Change	Total 1972	Percent Change	Total 1972	Percent Change
LOSS3070	6,218	56	62,475	-30	225	2
LOSS4070	6,312	145	58,773	- 7	218	47
LOSS5070	4,808	181	37,631	3	160	70
LOSS6070	9,271	192	68,484	14	325	91
GAIN6070	10,827	228	90,944	13	366	92
GAIN5070	4,017	245	30,862	21	140	115
GAIN4070	4,231	188	27,613	10	147	90
GAIN3070	37,071	346	230,497	46	1,256	175
ALL NONMET.	82,755	222	607,279	13	2,837	99
TOTAL U.S.	367,232	280	1,912,871	30	12,498	118

Note: Retail Sales reported in millions of inflation corrected 1967 dollars
       Retail Employment reported in thousands of workers
       Percent Change represents change between 1929 and 1972

this gain is, it lagged behind the national sales gain of 280
percent, as well as behind the metropolitan gain of 301
percent.

Sales gains were not consistent either over time or across
population-change categories. Detailed data presented elsewhere (Johnson, 1980) indicate that retail sales stagnated
during the Great Depression and then grew rapidly during
and immediately after World War II. Following this postwar
expansion, aggregate nonmetropolitan retail sales began a
long, if perhaps unspectacular, period of growth. Such temporal fluctuations reflect the impact of nondemographic factors:
the stagnation of the thirties was largely a function of income
decrements during the Great Depression, and the rapid ex-

pansion of the forties was fueled by income gains and the pent-up consumer demand of the war.

Among such nondemographic factors, income changes are especially relevant, particularly in declining counties.[3] In the typical nonmetropolitan county, median family incomes increased by 115 percent (corrected for inflation) between 1949 and 1969. Given the paucity of income data before 1949, any effort to estimate income gains before then is difficult, but an increase of 20 percent between 1929 and 1949 is quite plausible.[4] Between 1929 and 1969, then, it is likely that median family income in a typical nonmetropolitan county rose by at least 135 percent, with a portion of that increase spent in the retail sector.

The total number of nonmetropolitan retail establishments increased by only 13 percent between 1929 and 1972, despite the substantial sales gains during the period. This increase was smaller than that for the nation as a whole, and lagged far behind the 39 percent increase in establishments achieved in metropolitan areas. Over 1.9 million retail units served the country in 1972. As sales gains alone were not enough to increase the number of establishments significantly, the increases in demand for retail goods had to be accommodated in other ways.

Nationwide, retail employment more than doubled between 1929 and 1972, to over 12.5 million. The greatest gains were achieved in metropolitan areas (125 percent); nonmetropolitan retail employment increased by 99 percent during the period. Such gains are smaller than those for sales, but greater than those for units.

Surprisingly, gains in retail sales were common whether a county gained or lost population. Even among the 478 counties that lost population continuously from 1930 to 1970, median sales grew by 40 percent (Table 3.2), despite the fact that a typical county in this group had 38 percent fewer residents in 1970 than in 1930. Nonetheless, there was a clear linkage between the direction, duration, and magnitude of population change and retail growth. The most impressive gains by far occurred among extended-growth counties. Retail gains in this group exceeded the national average as well as the retail

TABLE 3.2
Median Population in 1970, Population Change 1930 to 1970, Retail Activity Levels 1972, and Retail Change 1929 to 1972 by County Group for All Nonmetropolitan U.S. Counties

	Population			Retail Sales per County		Number of Units per County		Number of Retail Employees per County	
	Number of Counties	Median 1970	% Change 1930-70	Median 1972[a]	% Change 1929-70	Median 1972	% Change 1929-72	Median 1972	% Change 1929-72
LOSS3070	478	7,955	-38	9,162	40	106	-30	341	-3
LOSS4070	373	11,722	-20	12,493	144	129	-7	436	44
LOSS5070	164	15,812	-5	21,349	173	189	5	695	64
LOSS6070	273	15,774	-8	21,768	156	192	8	797	75
GAIN6070	441	14,002	-2	18,686	237	171	17	613	91
GAIN5070	142	15,815	20	21,154	232	172	18	742	106
GAIN4070	80	24,267	25	43,143	196	268	16	1,448	99
GAIN3070	474	36,950	56	61,659	367	412	48	2,062	178
ALL NONMET. COUNTIES	2,425	14,889	4	19,750	182	175	4	674	70
TOTAL U.S.	3,060[d]	66,328[c]	65[b]	120,010[c]	280[b]	622[c]	30[b]	4,061[c]	96[b]

[a] All sales figures are corrected for inflation and reported in thousands of 1967 dollars
[b] Figures for Total U.S. represent aggregate percentage changes
[c] Figures for Total U.S. represent total value for U.S. divided by the numbers of counties
[d] Total counties in continental U.S. 1970

gains registered in many metropolitan counties. Among the county groups with mixed periods of population growth and decline, retail gains were substantially greater than for the long-term losers but less spectacular than among consistent gainers.

Unlike changes in sales, changes in the number of retail establishments serving a county coincided closely with population shifts. Protracted-decline counties lost the most units, whereas extended-gain counties gained the most. In general, changes in the number of units were much smaller than shifts in sales. For example, among counties that gained population continuously, the number of retail units increased by only 48 percent despite a sales gain of 367 percent. Clearly, a substantial increase in sales was required just to retain the number of units existing in 1929. In counties where sales did not increase substantially (i.e., LOSS3070), the number of units dropped significantly. In general, establishment shifts were similar in magnitude to those in population. Establishment change was in the same direction as population change but was less than proportionate, suggesting organizational resistance to change.

The pattern of change in numbers of employees falls between the two already considered. Although employee numbers are closely linked to the number of retail establishments in an area, under some conditions employment adjustments represent an alternative organizational response to changes in demand. Except among counties with continuous population loss, employment increased everywhere despite widespread reductions in the number of establishments. However, counties with the greatest population gains, and consequent increases in sales, also had the largest gains in retail employment. In contrast, protracted-decline counties tended to have the smallest employment gains.

Coping with Demand Shifts: Scale Adjustment and Resistance to Establishment Change

Despite the continual change in demand for retail goods that was caused by both population change and increased

TABLE 3.3
Comparative Percentage Change in the Number of Retail Units for Consistent Periods
of Population Change of Given Duration (in Percent)

	Duration of Consistent Population Change[a]			
	10 years	20 years	30 years	40 years
Unit change in direction opposite to population change	37	24	16	12
Unit change in same direction but greater than population change	45	34	32	30
Unit change in same direction but less than population change	18	42	52	58
	100(2,425)	100(1,711)	100(1,405)	100(952)

[a]Counties are included in each category that is relevant. For example, a county that
lost population consistently from 1950 to 1970 is included in both the 10 and 20
year categories.

per capita spending, the organizational structure in both growing and declining counties tended to resist change in the number of retail units. The increase in units did not keep pace with population increase in growing counties, nor did the number of units decrease as rapidly as population among declining counties.

Such resistance was not strong during the initial stages of population change. However, as the duration of consistent change increased, so did the percentage of counties with establishment change in the same direction as population change, but less than proportionate to it (Table 3.3). This pattern was well established by the time the process of consistent population change had been under way for thirty to forty years. For example, 58 percent of the counties that lost or gained population consistently for forty years had establishment changes in the same direction as, but smaller in magnitude than, the population shift. Another 30 percent of these counties had establishment changes in the same direction as, but greater in magnitude than, those in population. Only 12 percent had a population gain and an establishment loss, or a population loss and an establishment gain.

These findings reinforce earlier fragmentary evidence of local resistance to reductions in the number or availability of public or private functions in depopulated areas (Klietsch, 1962; Taves, 1961). The reasons for such resistance are not well understood, but economic factors certainly are involved. The financial commitments required to open a new unit or liquidate an existing one make capricious expansions or contractions of the local retail base unlikely. For example, small units continue to operate in declining counties, despite inadequate profit margins, because no resale market exists for them, and many owners would rather forego some income than lose their capital by abandoning the business (Taves, 1961). Because most retail units have an active proprietor, personal factors also contribute to the resistance to establishment change. Elderly proprietors often continue to run failing firms until they die or retire, because they have no other opportunities.

Demand shifts can be accommodated not only through adjustments in the number of retail units but also through adjustments in the scale of their operations—for instance, by hiring short-term employees and expanding shopping hours to accommodate the Christmas rush. The capacity of retail units to accommodate large fluctuations in demand by adjusting their scale of operations increases the system's resistance to proportionate adjustments in the number of units. Because retailing is labor intensive, businesses make scale adjustments primarily by manipulating the labor force. The large pool of low-wage, underemployed workers available in nonmetropolitan areas, coupled with the minimal skills required for entry-level retail work, makes it easy for establishments to adjust their scale of operations incrementally. In addition, scale expansion spreads the rising fixed cost of doing business over a greater total volume, thus retaining or increasing profit margins.

Such scale adjustments are measured by calculating the ratio of total retail sales to the number of establishments and by determining the mean number of retail employees per establishment. Incremental gains in either of these measures suggest that the typical unit in the county is expanding its scale of operations, whereas reductions indicate a contracting scale. Studied over time, such measures reflect the second

TABLE 3.4
Median Values of Selected Measures of Retail Activity in 1972 and Percentage
Change 1929 to 1972 by County Group

	Retail Sales per Capita		Retail Sales per Unit		Employees per Unit		Residents per Unit	
	1972	Percent Change	1972	Percent Change	1972	Percent Change	1972	Percent Change
LOSS3070	1,141	124	87,000	95	3.3	39	77	-13
LOSS4070	1,112	205	97,000	165	3.4	55	87	-16
LOSS5070	1,367	191	113,000	173	3.9	61	85	-12
LOSS6070	1,487	125	116,000	128	4.2	60	80	2
GAIN6070	1,340	253	108,000	194	3.6	63	83	-17
GAIN5070	1,397	168	116,000	185	4.1	75	88	0
GAIN4070	1,671	116	141,000	164	4.6	72	84	14
GAIN3070	1,659	171	153,000	210	5.2	86	92	14
ALL NONMET.	1,351	170	114,000	164	3.8	62	84	- 7
TOTAL U.S.	1,807	128	192,000	193	6.5	69	106	28

Note: All sales figures are corrected for inflation and reported in 1967 dollars
       Percent Change is the percentage change between 1929 and 1972
       Total U.S. figures for 1972 are means rather than medians
       Percent Change for Total U.S. represents the aggregate percent change for
         the nation

major avenue of the infrastructure's reaction to change in the demand for goods.

The widespread resistance to adjustments in the number of retail units proportionate to population change explains many of the differences among county groups in organizational responses to demand shifts. For example, in the protracted-decline counties there was a decrease in the total number of retail units, despite a significant rise in per capita retail spending fueled by rising incomes (Table 3.4). The substantial loss of population from such counties was certainly a primary factor in the loss of units. Such unit losses were coupled with a moderate increase in the scale of operations of the surviving units, evident in the 1972 ratios of both sales per unit and employees per unit. Although these ratios remained lower in protracted-decline counties than in other county groups, the scale of operations in the remaining units was still substantially larger than it had been in 1929. Nevertheless, losses in retail units were not proportionate to population losses, a fact that partly explains the relatively low sales volume, small number of workers, and declining population per unit in protracted-decline counties[5]—in short, a smaller scale of operations than would otherwise have been expected. Note that the increase in per capita sales was greater than that in per establishment sales in all but the most recently declining counties, just the opposite of what happened in growing counties.

The greatest scale expansion occurred in protracted-growth counties, where resistance to adding establishments meant that units had to handle more volume to accommodate the growing and more affluent population. The result was a substantial increase in workers, sales, and population per establishment. In short, a more than proportionate increase in the scale of operations was necessary to offset a less than proportionate increase in the number of units; per establishment sales increased faster than per capita expenditures in all but the most recently growing counties.

There are two possible organizational responses to a change in the demand for services. The first, and certainly the most expedient, is to adjust the scale of operations of units. Such scale adjustments can occur with minimal impact on the organizational structure itself. The second and more fundamental adjustment is to change the actual number of units providing retail services. Because such change requires the creation or dissolution of units, it occasions significantly more severe readjustments on the part of the organization and the population served. The two adjustment mechanisms are not mutually exclusive; in fact, the data indicate that both play a role in the organizational response.

It is important to emphasize the similarity in responses to both growth and decline. In either case there was resistance to a change in the number of units proportionate to the change in population. There was in most cases some adjustment in the number of units, and in the appropriate direction. But the change was not proportionate to the change in population, and in both growing and declining counties further adjustments occurred through manipulation of the scale of operations. For both growing and declining counties the result was an expansion in scale, but among declining counties the increment was less than would have been expected given the per capita spending gains. In growing county groups the upward adjustment was more than proportionate to increased per capita spending.

The Impact of Population Change on Specific Types of Retail Functions

Retail units may be grouped into two major segments according to the type of goods they provide. The first provides convenience goods needed frequently, such as groceries, gasoline, and hardware. Lower volume, higher priced goods required less frequently are supplied by units in the shopping goods segment.[6]

Fewer convenience and shopping goods establishments served a declining county in 1972 than in 1954, with the incidence and severity of the reductions increasing as the period of consistent population loss lengthened (Table 3.5). In general, 72 percent of the counties that lost population consistently from 1950 to 1970 also lost establishments. In spite of greater sales gains in the shopping goods segment, 75 percent lost shopping outlets, while 67 percent lost convenience units. As a result, sales per establishment increased more rapidly in the shopping goods segment, and the traditional pattern of many small convenience outlets and fewer, larger shopping goods outlets became more pronounced during the period. However, this conclusion is suggestive rather than definitive, because data are missing for a large number of counties.

The number of convenience establishments grew in 75 percent of the counties that gained population consistently from 1950 to 1970, reflecting the sensitivity of the convenience goods segment to shifts in the proximate customer base. Although 65 percent of the growing counties added shopping units, the rate of addition of these units was slower. This trend, combined with greater gains in consumer expenditures

TABLE 3.5

Median Percentage Change in Population 1950 to 1970, Income 1949 to 1969, and Retail Activity in the Convenience and Shopping Clusters 1954 to 1972 by County Group

County Group	Pop. Chg. 1950-1970	Inc. Chg. 1949-1969	Convenience Goods			Shopping Goods		
			Sales[a]	Units	Sales/[a] Unit	Sales[a]	Units	Sales/[a] Unit
LOSS3070	-22%	97%	3%	-17%	22%	17%	-21%	35%
LOSS4070	-18%	125%	27%	- 4%	33%	34%	-14%	49%
LOSS5070	-16%	90%	42%	- 3%	46%	39%	-12%	52%
LOSS6070	- 2%	88%	14%	- 2%	17%	33%	- 6%	37%
GAIN6070	- 1%	153%	71%	14%	52%	63%	5%	54%
GAIN5070	15%	130%	54%	13%	42%	71%	9%	59%
GAIN4070	22%	104%	40%	8%	40%	61%	11%	52%
GAIN3070	27%	115%	69%	19%	45%	82%	12%	62%
ALL NONMET.	- 4%	115%	51%	- 4%	51%	43%	2%	39%
Total U.S.[b]	35%	98%	61%	10%	46%	92%	13%	71%

[a]Data are available only for roughly 50% of all the counties on this item. Thus the reported figures should be interpreted with extreme caution.

[b]Total U.S. figures report percentage change for the nation as a whole rather than medians.

for shopping goods, led to a more rapid increase in the total sales per establishment in the shopping goods segment. As a result, the size gap between convenience and shopping goods outlets widened.

Earlier researchers (Doeksen, et al., 1974; Bollinger, 1972) discovered that rural people now prefer to shop in places where a variety of retail establishments provide a wider selection of goods and price competition among merchants. The increased mobility and affluence of the rural population lead many of them to bypass small local retail centers, where rural people traditionally shopped, and travel to larger regional shopping centers. Data not presented here indicate that retail losses were most severe in declining counties without a large urban place, and gains were greatest among growing counties that contained an urban place of over 10,000. This pattern held among counties regardless of their adjacency to metropolitan areas.

The trend toward shopping in larger places was stronger in the shopping goods segment, in which the high price and infrequent need for goods made individuals more willing to travel longer distances to obtain them. The frequent demand for most convenience goods appears to have constrained consumers to seek them in establishments close to home. In counties that lost population, retailers of high-priced items suffered the most because they faced both increasing competition from distant centers and a declining local market (Bollinger, 1972). Over 70 percent of the protracted-decline counties suffered a net loss of shopping goods units between 1954 and 1972. Generally, the trend in the shopping goods segment was toward fewer, larger units concentrated in regional shopping centers. The growing number of high-volume, chain department stores in nonmetropolitan areas exemplifies this trend. In many counties, other general merchandisers trying to compete with such department stores suffered particularly severe losses (Johnson, 1980).

Organizational innovations such as the supermarket and department store also affected the retail sector, for such units combined functions formerly provided by several establishments into a single operating entity. Although both department stores and supermarkets existed before 1954, their diffusion to nonmetropolitan areas was delayed until rising rural mobility and affluence created an adequate customer base to support them. Once established, these units supplanted many smaller, specialized outlets. For example, the long-term decline in the number of food stores during the study period can be explained in part as a function of the widespread diffusion of supermarkets to nonmetropolitan areas.

The Causal Impact of Population Change on Retail Trade

In order to ascertain the impact of population change on the retail infrastructure, I have developed a path analytic model to specify and estimate empirically the relationship between population change and the several retail variables.[7] The model considers only the period from 1948 to 1972, becaue county-level income data were not available for earlier periods (Figure 3.1).[8]

The strong causal impact of population change (POP4870) on sales (SLE4870) is reflected in the substantial path coefficient linking them. Other things being equal, a growing population stimulated a rapid rise in sales. Population decline reduced, though it rarely eliminated such sales gains. This strong link between population and sales change, coupled with the latter's ties to employment and establishment change, confirms that change in sales mediated between population change and retail structure.

Income change (INC4969) is included as a second exogeneous variable, because retail activity depends not only on how many people there are, but also on how much they have to spend. The causal impact of income on sales is reflected in the large direct path linking them. Thus, as income gains diverged from the mean increase of 128 percent, they caused sales gains to diverge from the mean increase of 65 percent.[9]

Change in the number of establishments (EST4872) serving a county is the first of two endogeneous variables that represent the retail structure. Population change exerted the dominant

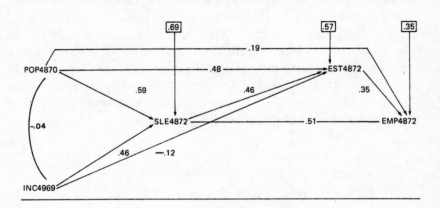

Where: POP4870 = Percentage change in population 1948 to 1970
         INC4969 = Percentage change in median family income corrected for
                   inflation 1949 to 1969
         SLE4872 = Percentage change in retail sales corrected for inflation 1948 to 1972
         EST4872 = Percentage change in number of retail establishments 1948 to 1972
         EMP4872 = Percentage change in retail employment 1948 to 1972

Matrix of Correlation Coefficients, Means, and Standard Deviations

	POP	INC	SLE	EST	EMP	MEAN	Std. Dev.
POP4870	–	-.04	.57	.75	.74	.8%	29.8
INC4969	-.04	–	.44	.06	.24	127.8%	61.8
SLE4872	.57	.44	–	.69	.86	64.8%	75.3
EST4872	.75	.07	.69	--	.85	-5.2%	27.1
EMP4872	.75	.21	.86	.85	–	15.0%	42.9

Note: Figures below diagonal are original correlations and those above are correlations
        reproduced from the reduced model.

        Analysis based on 2323 cases; 67 were eliminated because of missing data and 34
        as extreme outliers.

Figure 3.1   Path Diagram of Population Change and its Impact on the Retail Structure

causal influence on establishment change, with the impact
divided between a direct effect (.48) and an indirect effect
(.27).[10] This indirect effect occurs because population change
causes a sales shift that, in turn, precipitates an adjustment
in the number of units.

Sales change also exerts an independent causal influence
on unit change, aside from its part in mediating the impact
of population change. Sales change explains 10 percent of

the variance in establishment change, even after population and income change account for 57 percent.

The final endogeneous variable is the percent change in retail employment (EMP4872) between 1948 and 1972. Population change exerts a substantial causal impact on employment, as it does on the other retail variables; however, the bulk of population's effect is indirect, having been mediated through the sales and establishment variables. The indirect effect of population change on employment is .47.

Sales also has an independent causal impact on employment. The largest component of this effect is direct, although there is also an indirect effect through the establishment variable. The strong direct effect of sales on employment indicates that employment shifts were an alternative to opening or closing units. If the retail structure had responded to demand shifts solely by adjusting the number of units, and employment change had been simply a byproduct, there would have been no direct effect of sales on employment.

The final causal path links establishment and employment change. Although most of the bivariate correlation between them is attributable to causally prior variables, a change in the number of units in a county does exert a modest independent causal effect on employment. Such a finding is not surprising, however, because the opening or closing of a unit inevitably affects employment.

Thus, population change did exert a substantial causal impact on each of the three retail variables. In each case, population change was positively related to retail change, though the type of linkage varied. The effect of population on sales change was direct; its effect on the number of retail establishments was both direct and indirect; and its effect on employment change was mostly indirect, mediated through sales and employment change.

Income change exerted a significant causal impact on retail trade, quite independently of population change. Retail sales also exerted a unique and significant causal effect on both employment and establishment change. In addition, sales mediated much of the impact of population and income change on the employment and establishment variables. The substantial direct effect of sales on employment change is evidence of the roles of both employment and establishment change as mechanisms for organizational adjustment to shifting demand for retail services. Finally, establishment change also made a unique causal contribution to the explanation of employment change, indicating that it had a role beyond conveying the effects of sales and population change.

Estimating Population's Impact on Retailing

Although path analysis is valuable in elaborating the causal linkages among variables, an analysis of covariance using the general linear model provides better estimates of the general impact of population change on retailing. This approach maximizes the variance in the retail variables accounted for by population change, by disaggregating population change into three components representing the rate, duration, and direction (positive or negative) of change.[11] Equations provide estimates of the average annual change in retail sales, employment, and establishments for population change of a specific rate, duration, and direction.[12]

Using a linear model, we can determine whether the organizational response to population increase is symmetrical to that to decline—that is, whether a population increase of a given magnitude and duration elicits an organizational response opposite to that for a decline of the same magnitude and duration. If symmetry exists, it implies that the process by which the retail system expands to accommodate a growing population is reversed to adjust to a declining population. Such a finding would be contrary to ecological theory, which holds that system change is irreversible. In the ecological model, if an expanding system later contracts, it does so through a different process. Such a model implies that the retail response to growth will not be symmetrical to that for decline.

The nearly universal increase in sales between 1929 and 1972 is reflected in the regression model reported in Table

TABLE 3.6
Regression Estimates of the Average Annual Percentage Change in Retail Sales in
Response to Population Growth or Decline of a Given Magnitude and Duration (in Percent)

Duration of Consistent Population Change	Average Annual Rate of Population Change[a]					
	$-1\frac{1}{2}$%	-1%	$-\frac{1}{2}$%	$\frac{1}{2}$%	1%	$1\frac{1}{2}$%
10 years	1.21	1.75	2.30	3.90	4.12	4.33
20 years	1.20	2.05	2.90	4.91	5.34	5.78
30 years	1.19	2.34	3.50	5.91	6.57	7.22
40 years	1.18	2.64	4.09	6.92	7.79	8.67

$R^2 = .42$ $\qquad$ N = 2,354

[a]Regression equations used to predict the average annual rate of change in retail sales
were as follows:

For Growing Counties:
Avg. Annual Sales Change = 2.896 + -.005(POPCHG) + .079(DUR) + .044(DURPOP)

For Declining Counties:
Avg. Annual Sales Change = 1.940 + .484(POPCHG) + .090(DUR) + .061(DURPOP)

Where:
POPCHG   is the average annual rate of population change.
DUR   is the duration of consistent population change.
DURPOP   is an interaction term representing the joint effect of the rate and
         duration of population change. It was obtained by multiplying the
         rate of population change by the duration of change.

Note: For clarity of presentation, the prediction equations for growing and declining
        counties are reported separately here. The actual analysis used only a single
        equation.

3.6. Even in a county that lost 1.5 percent of its 1930 population
consistently each year for forty years, the expected annual
sales gain was 1.2 percent.[13] At the other extreme, the powerful
influence of population growth on sales is evident in the 8.7
percent annual sales increase expected for counties that gained
1.5 percent of their 1930 population annually for forty years.

A regression model containing terms representing the direction, duration, and rate of population change plus the
interaction among these components provides the best prediction of change in sales. The longer the expected growth
or decline lasts, the higher is the expected annual sales gain.
This duration effect, in turn, is largely attributable to the
general rise in real income during the period. Information

TABLE 3.7
Regression Estimates of the Average Annual Percentage Change in Retail Establishments
in Response to Population Growth or Decline of a Given Magnitude and Duration (in Percent)

Duration of Consistent Population Change	Average Annual Rate of Population Change[a]					
	-1½%	-1%	-½%	½%	1%	1½%
10 years	-.64	-.46	-.28	.35	.48	.61
20 years	-.78	-.56	-.33	.35	.56	.76
30 years	-.93	-.65	-.38	.36	.63	.90
40 years	-1.07	-.75	-.42	.37	.71	1.05
		R^2 = .46			N = 2,370	

[a]Regression equations used to predict the average annual rate of change in retail
establishments were as follows:

For Growing Counties:
Avg. Annual Establishment Change = .273 + .131(POPCHG) + - .006(DUR) + .014(DURPOP)

For Declining Counties:
Avg. Annual Establishment Change = -.111 + .254(POPCHG) + .0004(DUR) + .010(DURPOP)

Where:

POPCHG   is the average annual rate of population change.
DUR   is the duration of consistent population change.
DURPOP   is an interaction term representing the joint effect of the rate and
         duration of population change. It was obtained by multiplying the rate
         of population change by the duration of change.

about the direction of population change (represented by a dummy variable coded 1 for growth or 0 for decline) also improves the predictive power of the model, despite the fact that the rate variable has a sign. Although sales gains occurred whether a county grew or declined, both the rate of increase and the acceleration with extended duration were smaller among declining counties.

Unlike sales, the numbers of retail establishments varied in the same direction as population change, regardless of the latter's duration (Table 3.7). More important, establishment change in response to population gain was symmetrical to that for decline, for at every rate and duration a loss of population elicited the opposite response of a gain in population. For example, an annual population loss of 1.5 percent sustained for twenty years resulted in an annual establishment loss of .78 percent, whereas a population gain of the same rate and duration caused an establishment gain of .76 percent annually. Resistance to establishment change is reflected in predicted rates of unit change consistently lower than those in population. Clearly, the number of units serving a county is extremely sensitive to the number of patrons, regardless of how per capita spending levels change.

The pattern of establishment change was affected by the duration of consistent population change as well as by its rate. Counties that gained or lost population for extended periods experienced more rapid establishment change than counties in which consistent change was recent. The dummy variable representing the direction of change as well as the interaction terms do little to improve the prediction of establishment change. Thus, the establishment change in response to population change was symmetrical.

Employment change, on the other hand, was asymmetrical. Employment gains were common in counties experiencing moderate population loss, as well as among those that gained population (Table 3.8). Only when the average annual population loss exceeded 1 percent did employment levels decline. Moreover, in growing counties, the rate of employment change was more than proportionate to the rate of population change.

Employment patterns were affected by the direction and duration of population change, as well as by its rate. For growing counties, sustained population gains accelerated the rate of employment increase, reflecting the need to expand the scale of units to meet the spiraling demand for goods. Among declining counties, the duration effect was not as strong; however, prolonged decline did speed the rate of employment gain among counties with modest losses, or slow the rate of employment decline among those with severe losses.

The disparity between the responses of employment and establishments to population change is a function of their differential linkage to population and sales. The close tie between changes in population and changes in number of establishments made the latter less sensitive to fluctuations in sales. Thus, the number of units fell in declining counties, despite sales gains there. Given this tendency of population

TABLE 3.8
Regression Estimates of the Average Annual Percentage Change in Retail Employment
in Response to Population Growth or Decline of a Given Magnitude and Duration
(in Percent)

Duration of Consistent Population Change	Average Annual Rate of Population Change[a]					
	$-1\frac{1}{2}\%$	-1%	$-\frac{1}{2}\%$	$\frac{1}{2}\%$	1%	$1\frac{1}{2}\%$
10 years	-.61	-.22	.17	1.11	1.34	1.57
20 years	-.56	-.06	.44	1.66	2.02	2.38
30 years	-.51	.10	.71	2.21	2.70	3.20
40 years	-.45	.26	.98	2.76	3.39	4.01
		$R^2 = .61$			$N = 2,354$	

[a]Regression equations used to predict the average annual rate of change in retail
employment were as follows:

For Growing Counties:
   Avg. Annual Employment Change = .461 + .194(POPCHG) + .042(DUR) + .026(DURPOP)

For Declining Counties:
   Avg. Annual Employment Change = .175 + .554(POPCHG) + .038(DUR) + .022(DURPOP)

Where:

   POPCHG is the average annual rate of population change.
   DUR   is the duration of consistent population change.
   DURPOP is an interaction term representing the joint effect of the rate and
           duration of population change. It was obtained by multiplying the
           rate of population change by the duration of change.

and unit change to covary, and given the resistance to proportionate unit adjustments, the major organizational response to the general sales increase had to occur through employment. The result was more retail employees entering the labor force in growing areas and in most declining ones. In counties that lost population, the modest increase in operational scale accomplished by hiring more workers allowed business to meet the increased retail demand despite reductions in the number of units. Likewise, the substantial expansion of the retail work force in growing counties provided the means to meet the demand surge with only a few additional units.

In sum, though the establishment reaction to population change was symmetrical, the employment reaction was not.

Because the general retail response is the combination of these two elements, the general response is asymmetrical. This asymmetry supports the ecological tenet that system change is irreversible. If a growing unit later contracts, it does so through a different process.

Summary and Conclusions

The retail data presented here confirm that population change cannot prevail for long without concomitant organizational adjustments. Structural adjustment became more pronounced as the magnitude and duration of consistent population change increased. Population change affected sales directly, and the number of establishments both directly and indirectly, through sales. Population change influenced employment largely indirectly, through sales and establishment change, though there was also a modest direct effect. Sales, though not a structural variable, played an important part in mediating between population change and the retail structure.

Aggregate sales increased regardless of a county's history of population change, but the increments were largest in counties that experienced protracted growth and smallest in those that experienced prolonged decline. Sales gains were widespread because rising income levels caused per capita retail expenditures to double. The organizational modification stimulated by population change included adjustments in both the number and the operational scale of units. Establishment adjustments were in the same direction as population change but less than proportionate to it, reflecting resistance to changing the number of units serving an area. Such resistance, coupled with rapidly rising retail demand, resulted in an expanded scale of operations among units in both growing and declining counties. These adjustments caused employment gains in all but the protracted-decline counties.

Although retailing in both growing and declining counties involved an increasing scale of operations and a growing retail labor force, population-decline counties were served by fewer of these larger units, whereas growing counties were served by more. The possibility of a symmetrical response, entailing both a reduced scale of operations and an absolute reduction in the number of units serving a declining county, was precluded by the economics of scale and by the demands of an increasingly mobile, affluent, and sophisticated, if somewhat smaller, clientele. The fact that no single process of organizational adjustment could account for the retail response to population change confirms the ecological expectation that the process of systematic expansion differs fundamentally from that of contraction.

Notes

1. The following represent the eight categories of retail functions enumerated by the Bureau of the Census in the Census of Retail Trade.

- Food Stores (SIC54). Includes grocery stores, meat markets, fruit and vegetable markets, candy stores, retail bakeries, and other food stores.
- Eating and Drinking Places (SIC58).
- Gasoline Service Stations (SIC54).
- General Merchandise Group (SIC53). Includes department stores, variety stores, and miscellaneous general merchandise stores.
- Automotive Dealers (SIC55, except 554). Includes motor vehicle dealers (new and used), auto and home supply stores, miscellaneous automotive dealers.
- Building and Hardware (SIC52). Includes building material and supply, hardware stores, retail nurseries, mobile homes.
- Apparel and Accessory (SIC56). Includes women's clothing, men's clothing, family clothing, shoe stores, and other apparel.
- Furniture, Home Furnishings and Equipment (SIC57). Includes furniture, home furnishings, household appliances, and radio and television.

2. I realize that relatively few retail units stayed in operation throughout the study period. The mortality rate for retail firms is quite high. Thus, adjustments in the scale of operations were often a function of newer, larger units replacing older, smaller units that

were no longer able to compete. The question of whether scale expansion occurred through adjustments in the size of existing units or through the replacement of existing units by new ones is itself quite interesting. Unfortunately, it cannot be addressed with the data available, nor is it particularly material to this research.

3. Although I do not here demonstrate that rising incomes caused retail sales to grow, there is strong evidence that the two are closely linked. Consumer expenditures on retail goods as a percentage of income remained stable or declined slightly between 1929 and 1972. Thus, as incomes rose, so did household expenditures on retail goods.

4. It is extremely difficult to estimate family income before 1949 because such data were not collected for a representative part of the population. Using data from *Historical Statistics of the United States: Colonial Times to 1970* (U.S. Bureau of the Census, 1975) for the nation as a whole, one can make a very rough estimate. For example, the mean family income of a sample of the U.S. population in 1929 was about $2,335.00 (in 1929 dollars). In later years median income tended to be about 75 to 80 percent of mean family income. Using that correction, and adjusting for inflation, real income increased by 133 percent between 1929 and 1969.

5. The finding that the median ratio of population per unit declined between 1929 and 1972 contradicts Johansen and Fuguitt (1979, 1984), who report an increase in the mean population per establishment between 1950 and 1970 in U.S. villages. Detailed review indicates that the median ratio declined among counties that lost population and increased among those that gained population. Resistance to proportionate unit adjustments was certainly a factor, but the findings also differed because of the unit of analysis. The county data presented here include open country residents who were a major clientele for village establishments. These data yield a population-to-establishment ratio of 80/1 at the county level, compared to 50/1 for the villages studied by Johansen and Fuguitt. As the open country population contracted, the retail customer base shrank. Where this contraction was not offset by population gains elsewhere in the county, the number of units also was likely to decline. The ratios used by Johansen and Fuguitt did not reflect this decline, because they are based on village population. In addition, many of the villages studied by Johansen and Fuguitt are shifting from rural business centers to residential centers, while retailing centralizes in larger population centers. The two studies also differ in their definitions of retailing and sources of data.

6. The shopping goods segment contains establishments selling items needed infrequently and includes the general merchandise, automotive dealers, apparel and accessory, and furniture and home furnishings categories of the Census of Retailing. The convenience segment includes all other retailers, most of whom sell goods needed frequently. Prominent among such retailers are food stores, eating and drinking places, gasoline service stations, building and hardware stores, and drug stores. Data on specific retail functions is not available in machine-readable form for the years before 1954. See Johnson (1980) for a more complete examination of the impact of population change on specific retail functions.

7. For those unfamiliar with causal analysis, a brief overview may be helpful. Causal analysis is a technique designed to delineate the structural relationships among variables, given a set of assumptions about the causal order of the variables. It assumes that the correlation between two variables is a function of either the causal impact of one on the other, or the causal impact of some antecedent variable or variables on both the original variables, or some combination of these two. One variable may affect another directly, or indirectly, or through a combination of direct and indirect effects. In the latter two cases, the influence of the causal variable is mediated by an intervening variable or variables. Thus, the primary purpose of causal analysis is to understand the linkages among variables, not to maximize explained variance. For the purposes of this book, population change is considered a causally prior (exogeneous) variable, and the subjects of investigation are the magnitude and character of its influence on retail sales, establishments, and employment.

8. Greenwood (1975) warns that simultaneity bias may occur when variables measuring change are used as predictors of a dependent variable also measuring change. Such bias is likely if ordinary least-squares regression is used to estimate parameters in a model, violating the assumption that the causal system is recursive. It is not likely here because the model does not seriously violate the recursive assumption. It might be argued that a nonrecursive model with a feedback loop linking retail employment and population change would be more appropriate. Certainly abundant retail jobs enhance an area's appeal, while fewer retail opportunities inhibit population retention or gain; but, as Johansen and Fuguitt (1979) suggest, the proportion of the local labor force dependent on retailing is small in most nonmetropolitan counties. Thus,

incremental shifts in retail employment would have only minimal impact on population change.

High correlations among several independent variables also suggest that the data should be examined for multicollinearity, although multicollinearity is a potential problem primarily when sample data are used, and may not be relevant to this analysis of all nonmetropolitan counties. In any event, the Haitovsky test recommended by Rockwell (1975) proved insignificant, suggesting that the likelihood of multicollinearity is minimal; the standard errors of the regression coefficients were small; and analysis of samples of the counties consistently replicated the original path model. There is thus no evidence of multicollinearity.

Finally, the appropriateness of observing change over a single long interval has been questioned. Disaggregating the data into shorter intervals does cause some differences in the magnitude of the coefficients, but the general structure of the model remains largely unchanged.

9. No data are available on the extent of retail shopping outside the county by county residents. In an effort to provide an estimate of nonlocal shopping, I have used a surrogate measure. For 1960 and 1970 the Census Bureau reported the percentage of the labor force of each county that worked outside the county. If counties with a greater percentage of their labor force employed outside the county are also likely to have more extralocal shopping, then the commuting measure can be employed as a surrogate for extralocal shopping. Such an assumption is not unreasonable, because the mobility needed to work in a distant area would also allow shopping there. In addition, the attractive power of a distant area for employment may well be correlated with its attractive power for shopping. Thus, it is possible that by measuring change in the percentage of residents employed outside the county, one might also produce a rough estimate of the percentage change in nonlocal shopping.

When change in extralocal employment is added as an exogenous variable to a model linking population change 1958–1970 with the retail variables 1958–1972, it has no effect. The path coefficients for the commuting variable are all less than .05. If the commuting variable is a valid surrogate for extralocal shopping, then one must conclude that it adds little to the explanatory power of the model. Such a finding is consistent with Lord's (1982) report that while outshopping is a significant factor in some counties, the proportion of shopping outside the county of residence has probably not changed much in the past several decades.

10. Indirect effects are determined by tracing the various causal paths by which an independent variable can influence a dependent variable. For example, population change influences establishment change both directly (.48) and indirectly, because population change results in sales change, which, in turn, stimulates establishment change. The indirect effect is calculated by multiplying the impact of population change on sales change (.59) by the influence of sales change on establishment change (.46). This is equal to an indirect effect of .27. A similar procedure is used to calculate the indirect influence of population change on employment change. This latter calculation is more complicated because of the multiple indirect paths linking population change and establishment change.

11. The three components of population change used in the regression models were defined as follows:

Rate   = the average annual percentage change in population calculated over the entire period of consistent change. (Note that a sign is attached to the rate variable, so a county that lost population will have a negative rate.)

Duration = number of years of consistent population change.

Direction = a dummy variable indicating whether the county lost or gained population. For each county, only data for the consistent period of population change ending in 1970 are included.

12. Tables 3.6 to 3.8 examine the impact of population change of a given direction, duration, and magnitude on the retail variables, in order to determine whether the response to growth is symmetrical to that to decline. Symmetry is tested by comparing regression estimates for growing counties with those for counties declining at the same rate for the same duration. Thus, the key elements are the estimated values for the dependent variables and the magnitude of R^2, neither of which is affected by multicollinearity. Detailed examination of individual partial regression coefficients is neither necessary nor appropriate.

13. In order to make these regression estimates, I assigned counties to groups on the basis of the duration of consistent

population change, and calculated the average annual rate of change in population and each of the retail components with the following formula:

Average Annual $=$ $(((\text{1972 Value} - \text{Prior Value})) \div \text{duration}) \times 100$
Rate of Change $\qquad$ Prior Value

where: 1972 value= total value for 1972 (i.e., total establishments, 1972);

prior value= total value at beginning of period of consistent change (i.e., total establishments, 1939);

duration = number of years of consistent change (i.e., 32 years).

I then used these data to obtain the regression coefficients presented in the prediction equations.

4
Population Trends
and the Provision
of Services
in Rural Areas

The service industry has been among the fastest growing segments of the nation's economy in recent decades, with gains far exceeding even the impressive expansion of retailing. Service establishments derive the bulk of their revenues from the provision of services to the public rather than from the sale of merchandise. The functions they perform are an integral part of the general infrastructure that provides the local population with many of the necessities of everyday life.

Though the services considered here represent only a portion of those required by residents, they are, for the most part, dependent on the patronage of residents, and are therefore sensitive to local population shifts. Findings about structural adjustments within the service sector that have been stimulated by population change yield important information on the general systemic response to population change.

Though retailing and services are both sensitive to local population shifts, and have traditionally been combined in research on the linkage between changes in population and local infrastructure, there are good reasons to consider the service sector separately. For one thing, the surge in service activity between 1939 and 1972 exceeded the substantial retail gains of the same period by a wide margin, because the two sectors were at different developmental stages. Higher incomes contributed to this expansion (Zuiches and Price, 1980), as did technological and organizational innovations. Although retail expenditures increased as income rose, they did not increase as a proportion of total income, as did per capita spending on services. Entire new fields such as data processing developed, and, with the increasing complexity of electrical, refrigeration, and automotive equipment, people became much more dependent on skilled service personnel to install and maintain equipment in homes and businesses. In addition, as affluence and leisure time increased, people engaged in more recreation and entertainment away from home. These factors combined to generate enormous pressure for expansion of the service sector.

In contrast, retailing is a relatively mature field, and although it grew substantially during the period studied, it did not offer the same opportunities for the development of entirely new functions. Expansion in retailing was largely expansion of scale, or came through penetration into new geographic areas. What technological innovations there were came about through recombinations of existing activities to achieve economies of scale or market advantage (e.g., department stores, supermarkets, fast food restaurants, enclosed shopping centers).

Perhaps because its expansion was largely a matter of scale, the maturing retail sector became increasingly capital dependent. Particularly with the widespread advent of franchising and chain stores, the costs of opening a retail outlet have risen dramatically. True, many retail outlets still open on shoestring budgets. The high retail failure rate attests to the continuing efforts of underfinanced proprietors to enter an increasingly competitive arena. But retailing is no longer the last frontier of the entrepreneur; it is increasingly dominated by large corporations operating through chains of well-financed franchise or company-owned units. In contrast, many services can still be provided by individuals or small firms, often with relatively little start-up capital. The entry of new firms into the immature service industry is easier both because it is less expensive and because of the rapid creation of entirely new services. By considering these two sectors separately, we can contrast the adjustments to population change in parts of the local infrastructure at very different stages of development.

Other factors also argue against consolidation. The service sector is much smaller than retailing, particularly in nonmetropolitan areas. In 1972, nonmetropolitan expenditures on retail trade were eight times greater than expenditures on services, despite the latter's rapid expansion in the preceding decades. Individual service units are also much smaller than their retail counterparts. In 1972, the typical nonmetropolitan service establishment had $19,000 in receipts, compared to $114,000 for a retail unit (Johnson, 1980). Also, historically, service activity has been more concentrated in urban centers than has retailing (Bender, 1980). For example, in 1972, when 26 percent of the population resided outside metropolitan areas, 22 percent of retail sales, but only 12 percent of service receipts, accrued from nonmetropolitan counties. In part, the urban concentration of services reflects lower nonmetropolitan incomes as well as the traditional self-reliance of rural people, but the demand for certain services is still largely metropolitan. Business services, in particular, are heavily concentrated in large cities. Thus, the earlier developmental stage, smaller size, and different geographic distribution of the service industry make it inappropriate to combine the service sector with the larger, more developed retail sector.

Data and Procedure

The services examined here are those enumerated in the Census of Selected Service Industries.[1] These establishments derive the bulk of their revenues from providing services to the public rather than from the sale of merchandise. The Bureau of the Census has collected information on a portion of the service industry since 1939. Establishments included provide business, repair, and personnel services, as well as lodging and entertainment. Important omissions include any services provided by government, charitable, or religious institutions, as well as most health care services.[2] Data are from the statistical compendia developed by the Census Bureau and distributed between 1954 and 1972 as the *County and City Data Book*. Such data are supplemented with information from the decennial Census of Population for 1930 through 1970 and from the 1939 and 1972 Census of Business.

Countywide service activity is represented by three variables that parallel those reported for retailing: receipts, establishments, and employment. Much of the influence of population change on the service infrastructure is mediated through receipts (the total volume of service receipts, corrected for inflation). A change in the local population will affect service receipts, which in turn will cause adjustments in the numbers of employees and establishments in the area. Although the capital expenses involved in opening or closing a service establishment are less than those in retailing (especially when health services are excluded from consideration), the number of establishments is still less sensitive to short-term fluctuations than the number of employees. (As in the chapter on retailing, the term "employees" here includes partners and proprietors of unincorporated businesses, as well as paid employees of all firms.) Again, as in retailing, adjustments in the number of units and in the number of employees are to some extent alternatives, but drastic population change requires adjustment in both dependent variables.

Population Change and Its Impact on the Service Sector

The service sector grew rapidly between 1939 and 1972. In 1939, aggregate U.S. service receipts were only 8.1 billion dollars (in constant 1967 dollars). By 1972, they reached 90 billion dollars (Table 4.1)—an increase of over 1000 percent. Part of the increase is a function of Census Bureau revisions in the definition of the service sector, but the bulk of it represents real growth in service spending. Nonmetropolitan service receipts grew from 1.3 billion dollars in 1939 to 10.6 billion dollars in 1972. This represents a gain of over 700

TABLE 4.1
Total Service Receipts, Establishments, and Employment 1972 and Percentage Change
in these Components between 1929 and 1972 by County Group for Nonmetropolitan and
All U.S. Counties.

	Service Receipts		Service Establishments		Service Employment	
	Total 1972	Percent Change	Total 1972	Percent Change	Total 1972	Percent Change
LOSS3070	629	298	38,234	24	69	31
LOSS4070	626	385	33,121	43	67	56
LOSS5070	529	545	21,795	86	54	116
LOSS6070	1,193	623	44,913	102	118	162
GAIN6070	1,276	673	57,203	92	132	132
GAIN5070	638	1,081	19,968	125	59	269
GAIN4070	593	841	19,675	142	54	216
GAIN3070	5,157	1,004	165,031	197	480	303
ALL NONMET.	10,641	729	399,940	110	1,033	176
TOTAL U.S.	90,376	1,010	1,590,248	146	6,007	277

Note: Service Receipts reported in millions of inflation corrected 1967 dollars
Service Employment reported in thousands of workers
Percent Change represents change between 1939 and 1972

percent, somewhat smaller than the gain for the nation as a whole and significantly less than that in metropolitan areas.

The number of service establishments also increased during the period, although the incremental increases were much smaller than for receipts. Nationwide the number of service establishments increased by 146 percent, to 1.6 million, by 1972. As in the case of receipts, the greatest gains accrued to metropolitan areas. Nonmetropolitan gains were somewhat smaller (110 percent), but still represented a significant aggregate gain, from 190,000 units in 1939 to 400,000 in 1972.

The general trend in service employment was also upward, with gains greater than those in the number of establishments, but much small than those in receipts. By 1972 over 6 million workers were employed in the selected services enumerated by the Census Bureau. This represents a gain of 277 percent from the 1.75 million employed in the sector in 1939. Nonmetropolitan service employment exceeded 1 million by 1972, having grown by 176 percent since 1939.

The course of growth, however, was not steady (Johnson, 1980). During World War II and in the immediate postwar period, service receipts did not increase much above prewar levels in nonmetropolitan areas, though they did increase substantially elsewhere in the country. As a consequence, both service employment and the number of service establishments declined during and immediately after World War II. Service activity then grew rapidly during the 1950s and 1960s in both metropolitan and nonmetropolitan areas. The postwar expansion of retailing was more immediate than that in the service industries, particularly in nonmetropolitan areas; consumers initially devoted more of their discretionary income to obtaining long rationed goods, rather than services.

Service receipts grew in each county group; gains were greatest in counties with protracted population growth, but were substantial even among counties that lost population consistently for decades (Table 4.2). The systematic relationship between a county's history of population change and the magnitude of its service receipts gain is the first evidence of the causal impact of population change on the service industry.

The universality of the gains, however, implies that other factors also influence service activity—most prominently, increased personal income. Between 1949 and 1969 median family income (corrected for inflation) increased by 115 percent in the typical nonmetropolitan county. The additional discretionary income such gains produced permitted greater per capita spending on services. In declining counties, rising per capita spending more than offset revenue losses due to shrinkage of the customer base. And in counties with prolonged population increase, rising per capita spending combined with a growing customer base to stimulate enormous gains in service spending.

TABLE 4.2
Median Population 1970, Population Change 1930 to 1970, Selected Service Activity Levels 1972, and Selected Service Change 1939 to 1972 by County Group for All Nonmetropolitan U.S. Counties

	Population			Service Receipts Per County[a]		Number of Units Per County		Number of Service Employees Per County	
	Number of Counties	Median 1970	% Change 1940-1970	Median 1972	% Change 1939-1972	Median 1972	% Change 1939-1972	Median 1972	% Change 1939-1972
LOSS3070	478	7,955	- 31	849	291	62	21	106	30
LOSS4070	373	11,722	- 27	1,154	395	69	39	132	46
LOSS5070	164	15,812	- 9	1,967	547	103	87	245	117
LOSS6070	273	15,774	- 4	2,636	589	117	99	280	133
GAIN3070	441	14,002	- 6	1,860	636	101	86	213	114
GAIN4070	142	15,815	11	2,598	805	106	126	247	180
GAIN5070	80	24,267	31	4,379	771	183	142	482	201
GAIN6070	474	36,950	42	7,780	920	277	193	736	256
ALL NONMET. COUNTIES	2,424	14,889	- 7	2,050	545	104	82	227	113
TOTAL U.S.	3,060[d]	66,328[c]	54[b]	29,535[c]	1,010[b]	519[c]	146[b]	1,963[c]	277[b]

[a] All receipts are corrected for inflation and reported in thousands of 1967 dollars
[b] Figures represent aggregate percentage changes
[c] Figures represent total value for U.S. divided by the number of counties
[d] Total counties in continental U.S. 1970

The development of new services, rising demand for maintenance of complex equipment, and changing life styles also stimulated service spending. These factors, however, probably affected all counties in roughly the same way. Population change exerted a far more differential influence. It accelerated the receipt gains in growing counties and limited them in declining counties, and as the duration of consistent change increased, so did its impact on receipt gains.

The median number of service-providing units also increased in each county group, though the gains were smaller than for receipts. Population growth, particularly if it was protracted, substantially increased the rate of establishment gain, while population decline dampened it. Given the substantial increases in the volume of receipts, actual decline in the number of establishments was rare. But without consistent population increase, a high rate of establishment gain could not be sustained. And, because unit gains were less than proportionate to those for receipts, the operational scale of service outlets inevitably increased.

Given the labor-intensive nature of the service industry, the spiraling demand for services, and the increased number of service establishments, it is not surprising that the service labor force grew in nearly every county. The rate of employment increase was somewhat higher than that for establishments but lagged behind receipts. The magnitude of such employment gains is closely tied to local population trends. Thus, the labor force grew most in extended-growth counties, and only modestly in protracted-decline counties. Even if gains in receipts were substantial, employment increments were not significant unless accompanied by population gain.

Infrastructure Adjustments to Service Demand Shifts

To understand how the service infrastructure responded to population change, we must examine not only the individual performance of the service sector variables, but the interrelations among them. Per capita spending on services rose precipitously whether a county gained or lost population between 1939 and 1972 (Table 4.3). Rising incomes contributed

TABLE 4.3
Median Values of Selected Measures of Service Activity in 1972 and Percentage
Change 1939 to 1972 by County Group

	Receipts per Capita		Receipts per Unit		Employees per Unit		Residents per Unit	
	1972	Percent Change	1972	Percent Change	1972	Percent Change	1972	Percent Change
LOSS3070	113	469	13,966	224	1.7	5	121	-44
LOSS4070	109	554	16,234	241	1.8	4	160	-49
LOSS5070	138	650	19,359	254	2.1	15	148	-53
LOSS6070	173	542	21,207	247	2.3	26	120	-46
GAIN6070	132	674	17,775	288	1.9	10	137	-50
GAIN5070	149	617	21,621	305	2.2	32	123	-49
GAIN4070	200	502	24,060	269	2.3	27	136	-44
GAIN3070	200	574	26,984	258	2.7	30	135	-49
ALL NONMET.	141	561	19,000	251	2.1	15	134	-48
TOTAL U.S.	445	671	56,831	351	4.2	53	128	-37

Note: All Receipts figures are corrected for inflation and reported in 1967 dollars
        Percent Change represents the percentage change between 1939 and 1972
        Total U.S. figures for 1972 are means rather than medians
        Percent Change for Total U.S. represents the aggregate percent change for
        the nation

to this increase, but the per capita gains far exceeded income gains, indicating that residents spent a larger proportion of their incomes on services. The median per capita spending on services rose from only $21 in 1939 to $141 in 1972. This sum was still far less than the $1351 per capita spent on retail goods, but did represent a much more rapid rate of increase (561 percent, as against 170 percent for retailing). Generally, spending was higher among individuals in protracted-growth counties, but expenditures in most nonmetropolitan counties lagged behind those in metropolitan areas, indicating greater self-reliance, limited access to services, or simpler needs among nonmetropolitan residents and businesses. However, these differences were overshadowed by the sheer magnitude of the per capita spending gains, which were a principal factor in the tremendous expansion of the service sector.

Median receipts per establishment were smallest among long-term loss counties, and became progressively larger as the duration of loss shortened and loss was replaced by population gain. These differences in scale were substantial, with establishments in LOSS3070 typically having only about half the receipts volume of those in GAIN3070. Service establishments in nonmetropolitan areas were also significantly smaller than in the nation as a whole.

Despite these differences in scale, the rate at which receipts per establishment increased was roughly the same in each county group. In protracted-loss counties the rates of increase in service receipts and in per establishment service receipts were roughly equal. Thus, the total number of establishments did not increase very much, because most of the rising demand for services was absorbed through an increased scale of operations by a fixed number of units. But in the long-term growth groups the expansion of receipts per establishment was not sufficient to absorb the enormous gains in total receipts, so the number of establishments increased to meet the rapidly growing demand.

Unlike per unit receipts, the number of employees per unit remained relatively stable. What little growth there was occurred among counties with population gain. Thus the scale expansion in the service sector, unlike that in retailing, was accomplished without a significant increase in the number of employees per establishment. Increased worker productivity, shifts from part-time to full-time employment, and greater revenues for new services requiring technological expertise all contributed to the increase in receipts per worker.

The typical service establishment remained relatively small, handling a larger volume of receipts with a marginal increase in staff. Such modest scale expansion accommodated some of the rising demand for services. However, in most counties the number of establishments and employees also grew. These increases were greatest in the protracted-growth counties, where population gains multiplied the impact of rising per capita spending. In such counties, the small establishments that are characteristic of the service sector proliferated. Only in protracted-loss counties, where population declines dampened the effect of higher per capita spending, did the scale mechanism alone meet the demand surge. Thus, while demand for services increased almost everywhere, the magnitude of the gain depended on whether the population grew or declined.

The Causal Impact of Population Change on the Selected Services

The causal model presented here specifies and estimates empirically the relationship between population change and shifts in the structure of the service sector. Assigning population change an independent role oversimplifies a complex causal structure; however, because most of the services considered here depend on local patronage, they are sensitive to local population shifts.[3] Income change is included as a second exogeneous variable, but the absence of county-level income data before 1949 limits analysis to the period from 1948 to 1972.[4]

During this period, population change (POP4872) exerted a strong causal impact on service receipts (SLE4872) (Figure 4.1). A growing population increased the magnitude of the receipts gain. And, although a loss of population rarely caused an absolute decline in receipts, it slowed the rate of increase in comparison with that of a growing county.

The volume of service receipts also depends on how much residents have to spend, as is indicated by the moderately strong causal impact of income change (INC4969) on receipts. Income gains greater than the nonmetropolitan average caused higher levels of service spending than would be expected otherwise. However, income change had less impact on receipts than did population shifts. Together, population and income accounted for 23 percent of the variation in receipts, and the absence of a correlation between them suggests that each made an independent contribution.

Change in the number of establishments serving a county (EST4872) is the first indicator of organizational adjustment in the local service structure. Of the two exogeneous variables,

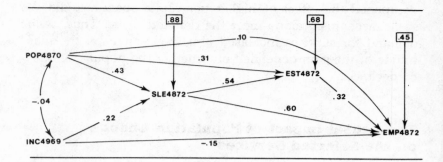

Where: POP4870 = Percentage change in population 1948 to 1970
         INC4969 = Percentage change in median family income corrected for inflation
                   1949 to 1969
         SLE4872 = Percentage change in service receipts corrected for inflation 1948 to 1972
         EST4872 = Percentage change in the number of service establishments 1948 to 1972
         EMP4872 = Percentage change in service employment 1948 to 1972

Matrix of Correlations, Means, and Standard Deviations

	POP	INC	SLE	EST	EMP	Mean	Std. Dev.
POP4870		−.04	.42	.54	.53	.6%	29.3
INC4969	−.04		.21	.10	.00	126.7%	60.5
SLE4872	.42	.21		.67	.82	431.8%	331.3
EST4872	.54	.14	.67		.76	171.9%	117.0
EMP4872	.53	.02	.83	.76		170.0%	145.1

Note: Figures below diagonal are original correlations and those above are correlations re-
        produced from the reduced model.

        Analysis based on 2193 cases;   131 were excluded because of missing data and 100
        because of extreme values.

Figure 4.1   Path Diagram of Population Change and its Impact on the Service Structure

population change had the strongest causal influence on how
many units provide services to a county. Most of this influence
was direct, but there was also a significant indirect effect
(.23) mediated through change in receipts. In contrast, income
change exerted a minimal indirect effect (.10) on establishment
change.

In addition to mediating the effects of population and
income on the establishment variable, change in the volume
of service receipts exerts an independent influence on change
in the number of service units. Its causal impact was equivalent
to that of population, and adding it to a model containing
population and income change increases the explained variance

from 23 percent to 53 percent. The independent contribution of the sales variable reflects the influence of a variety of other factors unrelated to population or income change.

Structural adjustments in the service sector are also reflected in changes in employment (EMP4872). The size of the service labor force did change in response to the ebbs and flows of population; however, most of population's effect was indirect (.43). The principal indirect path was through receipts, but population change also affected employment by causing establishment change. Income change exerted no net effect on employment, because the negative direct path was canceled by a positive indirect effect mediated by receipts.

Employment is particularly sensitive to changes in service receipts volume. Most of the effect was direct, though there was also an indirect effect (.17) because receipts-induced establishment change caused employment adjustments. The strong direct link between receipts and employment emphasizes the prominent role the latter played in absorbing the rising demand for services. Had this not been the case, most of the impact of receipts on employment would have occurred indirectly through the establishment variable, with employment changing because new units open. In fact, productivity gains allowed more activity to be handled by a given number of units, thereby weakening the relationship between changes in receipts and the need for additional units.

Establishment change also exerts a modest independent influence on employment. Though the bulk of the correlation between the variables was a function of causally prior variables, establishment change did uniquely account for 5 percent of the variation in employment. Thus, although employment shifts are to some extent an alternative to establishment change in coping with demand shifts, the two remain causally linked.

In sum, population change directly affects the volume of service receipts in a county. It also influences the number of units serving a county through the combination of a direct effect and an indirect effect mediated by receipts change. Finally, the impact of population change on service employment is largely indirect, with receipts and establishment change mediating the relationship. Thus, population change exerts a significant influence on the service infrastructure in a pattern quite similar to that reported for retailing.

Estimating the Impact of Population Change on the Services

This chapter uses a general linear model very similar to that presented for retailing, in order to make detailed estimates of the influence of population change on service receipts, establishments, and employment. This approach divides population change into three distinct components representing the separate influence of the rate, duration, and direction (positive or negative) of the change. The only difference between the analysis for retailing and that presented here is that data for services are available for only thirty years, as opposed to forty for retailing.

The widespread increase in service receipts is clearly evident in the predictions derived from the model that best represents the service receipts data. The model predicts substantial receipt gains even among counties with histories of sustained, heavy population losses. For instance, the model predicts that a hypothetical county that lost population at a rate of 1.5 percent per year for thirty years would have an average annual increase in service receipts of 9.8 percent (Table 4.4). Thus, even with a loss of 45 percent of its 1940 population by 1972, a sales gain of 294 percent would be expected for such a county. In comparison, the model predicts an average annual receipt gain of over 27 percent for a county with thirty years of consistent population growth of 1.5 percent per year. This rate would result in a total increase of 822 percent in service receipts for a county that had a population gain of 45 percent between 1940 and 1970. Clearly, coupled with the general factors stimulating a rising demand for the services considered here, such population gains generated enormous increases in service receipts in these growing counties.

The duration of consistent population change also had a substantial and universally positive impact on the pattern of

TABLE 4.4
Regression Estimates of the Average Percent Change in Service Receipts in Response
to Population Growth or Decline of a Given Magnitude and Duration (in Percent)

Duration of Consistent Population Change	Average Annual Rate of Population Change[a]					
	-1.5%	-1.0%	-0.5%	0.5%	1.0%	1.5%
10 years	5.54	6.57	7.60	9.37	9.65	9.93
20 years	7.67	9.52	11.37	16.41	17.54	18.67
30 years	9.81	12.47	15.13	23.46	25.43	27.40

R-square = .41   N = 2220

[a]Regression equations used to predict the average annual rate of change in service
receipts were as follows:
For Growing Counties:
   Avg. Annual Receipts Change = 2.88 + -1.12(POPCHG) + .62(DUR) + 1.69(DURPOP)

For Declining Counties:
   Avg. Annual Receipts Change = 4.06 + .44(POPCHG) + .46(DUR) + .16(DURPOP)

Where:
   POPCHG is the average annual rate of population change.
   DUR   is the duration of consistent population change.
   DURPOP is an interaction term representing the joint effect of the rate and
           duration of population change. It was obtained by multiplying the
           rate of population change by the duration of change.

Note: For clarity of presentation, the prediction equations for growing and declining
       counties are reported separately here. The actual analysis used only a single
       equation.

service receipts increase, with the expected rate of receipt
gain accelerating as the duration of consistent population
change was prolonged. The duration effect was greatest among
counties with protracted population gain and least among
counties with extended population decline. The model gains
additional increments in explanatory power by including direction and interaction terms, and we must therefore assume
that the response to population increase is essentially different
from the response to population decline.

The nearly universal increase in service receipts is also
evident in the predictions for establishment change, though
the gains are much more modest. For example, a county that
gained population consistently for thirty years at a rate of
1.5 percent a year is expected to have establishment gains
of 5.8 percent annually, or 174 percent over the thirty-year

TABLE 4.5
Regression Estimates of the Average Percent Change in Service Establishments in
Response to Population Growth or Decline of a Given Magnitude and Duration (in Percent)

Duration of Consistent Population Change	Average Annual Rate of Population Change[a]					
	−1.5%	−1.0%	−0.5%	0.5%	1.0%	1.5%
10 years	3.19	3.47	3.83	4.62	4.76	4.89
20 years	1.94	2.47	3.08	4.51	4.93	5.34
30 years	.64	1.47	2.33	4.40	5.10	5.79
		R-square = .30			N = 2261	

[a]Regression equations used to predict the average annual rate of change in service
establishments were as follows:

   For Growing Counties:
      Avg. Annual Establishment Change = 4.88 + -2.90(POPCHG) + -.04(DUR) + .06(DURPOP)

   For Declining Counties:
      Avg. Annual Establishment Change = 4.68 + .20(POPCHG) + -.05(DUR) + .05(DURPOP)

   Where:
      POPCHG is the average annual rate of population change.
      DUR   is the duration of consistent population change.
      DURPOP is an interaction term representing the joint effect of the rate and
             duration of population change. It was obtained by multiplying the
             rate of population change by the duration of change.

Note: For clarity of presentation, the prediction equations for growing and declining
       counties are reported separately here. The actual analysis used only a single
       equation.

period (Table 4.5). Although this is certainly a significant
gain, it hardly rivals the predicted receipts gain of over 800
percent for such a county. At the other extreme, counties
losing population at an annual rate of 1.5 percent for thirty
years are expected to gain establishments at a rate of only
.7 percent a year. In such counties the total predicted establishment gain of 21 percent also falls far short of the 300
percent gain expected in service receipts. The substantial
differences between receipts and establishment gains emphasize the expansion in the scale of operations of such
service units during the period.

The pattern of establishment change was affected by the
duration as well as the rate of consistent population change.
The duration effect was strongest among counties that lost

population, where the expected rate of establishment gain decelerated rapidly as population loss became prolonged. This deceleration is best exemplified in counties that lost population most rapidly. If such a loss was sustained for ten years, the model predicts an establishment increase of 3.2 percent annually, but if the loss continued for thirty years, the expected annual rate falls to only .7 percent. The duration effect on growing counties was generally the opposite of that for declining counties, tending to accelerate the rate of establishment gain. However, the duration effect on growing counties was much less pronounced, as is evidenced by the smaller differences in predictions for the various time periods. In fact, in some cases prolonging the period of population gain had only a minimal impact on the rate of establishment change. Thus, as population increase became prolonged, the rate of establishment gain accelerated modestly, but in the face of protracted population loss the rate of establishment gain decelerated rapidly.

The duration variable is not as useful in accounting for establishment change as in predicting receipts change. Nor is the direction variable very helpful. The relatively small incremental gains in explanatory power from including these variables suggest that the rate variable alone represents the data reasonably well. Such a finding implies that there is some symmetry in the establishment response to population change. However, there is no evidence of the nearly perfect symmetry evident in the model for retail establishments, where the duration and direction variables added almost nothing to the model.

The regression model for employment indicates that the number of service workers increased over time regardless of whether the population grew or declined. Nonetheless, population change did have a very consistent impact on employment. Employment gains were greatest among counties with substantial population growth sustained for several decades, and smallest among counties with heavy, prolonged population decline. A county that gained population at a rate of 1.5 percent per year for thirty years had a predicted annual employment gain of almost 8 percent per year, for a total of

TABLE 4.6
Regression Estimates of the Average Percent Change in Service Employment in Response to
Population Growth or Decline of a Given Magnitude and Duration (in Percent)

Duration of Consistent Population Change	Average Annual Rate of Population Change[a]					
	-1.5%	-1.0%	-0.5%	0.5%	1.0%	1.5%
10 years	1.90	2.45	3.00	3.48	3.73	3.97
20 years	1.35	2.12	2.89	4.86	5.41	5.95
30 years	.80	1.79	2.78	6.23	7.09	7.94

R-square = .39   N = 2,164

[a]Regression equations used to predict the average annual rate of change in service employment
were as follows:
  For Growing Counties:
    Avg. Annual Employment Change = 2.17 + -.12(POPCHG) + .11(DUR) + .06(DURPOP)

  For Declining Counties:
    Avg. Annual Employment Change = 3.44 + .66(POPCHG) + .01(DUR) + .04(DURPOP)

Where:
  POPCHG   is the average annual rate of population change.
  DUR   is the duration of consistent population change.
  DURPOP   is an interaction term representing the joint effect of the rate and duration
           of population change. It was obtained by multiplying the rate of population
           change by the duration of change.

Note: For clarity of presentation, the prediction equations for growing and declining
       counties are reported separately here. The actual analysis used a single equation.

238 percent over the thirty-year period (Table 4.6). At the other extreme, counties with an annual population loss of 1.5 percent sustained for thirty years had an expected annual employment gain of only .8 percent, or 24 percent for the entire period. Thus, even though population loss did reduce employment gains, the rapidly increasing demand for services still stimulated growth in the service labor force.

Adding a variable measuring the duration of consistent population change improves the predictions of employment change. As the duration of consistent population gain increased, the rate of employment gain accelerated substantially. In contrast, prolonged population decline led to a slight deceleration in the rate of increase in service employment. A duration effect was also evident in the establishment model, but in the employment data growing counties were affected the most by the duration of consistent population change, whereas in the establishment data it was the declining counties that were affected the most. For example, among counties with the greatest population losses, the rate of employment gain decelerated from 1.9 percent annually for consistent population decline of ten years' duration to only .8 percent for counties with consistent decline for thirty years, a net reduction of 1.1 percent. The rate of employment increase accelerated from 4.0 percent for counties with annual population gain of 1.5 percent for ten years to 7.9 percent for counties with consistent gain for thirty years, a net increase of almost 4 percent.

The regression data for employment also indicate a directional effect. A model expanded to include the direction and duration of population changes as well as the interaction between them, dramatically increases the explained variation over that obtained from a rate-only model. The incremental gains obtained by adding these terms are greater for the employment model than for the establishment model. Thus, there is no evidence of symmetry in the regression models estimating the employment response to population change.

The regression data for the services indicate that population change exerted a significant impact on each of the variables considered. However, there is no evidence of the intense resistance to establishment change evident in the retail sector, nor is there anything approaching the symmetry of response evident in the retail establishment response. In general, predicting the service sector reaction to population change requires complex regression models including terms reflecting the direction, duration, and interaction of the population terms, as well as the simple rate of population change. The need for such models implies that the service sector response to population increase was asymmetrical to its response to population decline.

A Comparison of Population's Impact on Retailing and Services

To facilitate comparisons of the retail and service sectors, I have recalculated the data for retailing, using 1939 as a

TABLE 4.7
Comparison of Changes in the Selected Service and Retail Sectors Between 1939 and
1972 by County Group

	Percent Change in Population	Percent Change in Sales		Percent Change in Units		Percent Change in Employment	
		Retail	Service	Retail	Service	Retail	Service
LOSS3070	-31	88	291	-35	21	- 3	30
LOSS4070	-27	146	395	-24	39	19	46
LOSS5070	- 9	187	547	-11	87	44	117
LOSS6070	4	160	589	-10	99	47	133
GAIN6070	- 6	254	636	- 4	86	64	114
GAIN5070	11	229	805	- 3	126	70	180
GAIN4070	31	260	771	6	142	89	201
GAIN3070	42	298	920	22	193	111	256
ALL NONMET.	- 7	186	545	-11	82	47	113
TOTAL U.S.	54	265	1010	8	146	75	277

Note: All sales figures are corrected for inflation and reported in 1967 dollars
        Percent Change represents the percentage change between 1939 and 1972
        Percent Change for Total U.S. represents the aggregate percent change for the
        nation

base year (Table 4.7). Total sales increased significantly in
each county group in both sectors for the period 1939 to
1972. And, in each sector, the magnitude of the gain depended
on the history of population change. Sales gains averaged
186 percent in the retail sector, compared to 545 percent in
the service sector. However, the aggregate expenditures on
retailing consistently exceeded those on services by a wide
margin.

In the retail sector, the establishment response to population
change was symmetrical; counties that lost population also
lost units, whereas those that gained population gained units.
In general, establishment change was in the same direction
as population change, but less, reflecting the strong resistance
to unit change that permeated the retail sector. In contrast,
the number of service establishments increased whether a

county's population grew or declined. Unit increases were smaller in counties losing population, but there is no evidence of resistance to unit changes similar to that in retailing.

Employment gains were common in both the retail and the service sectors, and occurred whether a county lost or gained population. Such gains were consistently larger in the service sector, but in each sector, the magnitude of the employment gain was heavily influenced by the size, duration, and direction of local population shifts.

The causal linkages between population change and adjustments in the organizational structure of the service sector are also similar to those reported for retailing. Such comparable patterning suggests that population change affects the infrastructure of each sector through a similar mechanism. However, the path coefficients and explanatory power of the models are consistently less for the service industry than for retailing, because the retail sector's maturity makes it more sensitive to shifts in the size of the local customer base than is the expanding service sector.

Apart from the rapid increase in service activity, the major difference between the sectors is in the pattern of establishment response to population shifts. In the retail sector, resistance to unit change, coupled with a symmetrical establishment response to population change, caused retail sales and employment to concentrate in larger units. In contrast, the number of service establishments and employees increased regardless of the history of population change in a county, though a loss of population did dampen the service gains. In the rapidly expanding service industry, the infrastructure response to demand shifts was nearly evenly balanced between adjustments in the number of establishments and changes in the number of employees. As a result, small units proliferated. This pattern is not apparent when the sector's are combined, as is common in most research on the subject.

Summary and Conclusions

The service industry data for nonmetropolitan counties confirm the human ecological expectation that population change stimulates concomitant adjustments in organizational structure. Such infrastructure adjustments become pronounced as the magnitude and duration of consistent population change increase. Population change directly affects the volume of service expenditures in a county; it influences the number of units serving a county both directly and indirectly; and it influences service employment largely indirectly. Changes in the volume of service receipts mediate much of the influence of population change on the service infrastructure. A population change causes receipts to grow at a faster or slower rate, which, in turn, influences the number of employees and establishments serving an area.

Between 1939 and 1972, expenditures on services increased substantially in nearly every county, despite the widespread incidence of prolonged population decline. The impact of population change on receipts is reflected in the fact that gains were smallest in protracted-decline counties and greatest in extended-gain ones. Gains in receipts were also stimulated by greater per capita spending on services as a result of rising incomes, changing lifestyles, and the proliferation of new services. In response to this enormous increase in expenditures, the number of both units and employees providing services grew in most counties. Population decline tempered this expansion; population increase accelerated it. The expansion occurred through a balanced increase in the number of units and employees, coupled with significant gains in worker productivity. Thus, the rising demand for services was accommodated by a proliferation of small units.

The general effect of population change on the service sector was not as strong as its effect on retailing; the rapid expansion of the immature service sector was less dependent on population change than was the slower growth of the more mature retail sector. The causal model representing the linkages between population change and adjustments in the service infrastructure is similar to that for retailing, but the general organizational responses in the two sectors differ. In the service sector there was a balanced increase of employment and establishments; in the retail sector establishment shifts were in the same direction as population change, but less than proportionate to it. This resistance to unit change caused scale expansion in the retail sector, as the labor force expanded to meet the growing demand for goods. Thus, structural adjustments in the service industry caused small units to proliferate, whereas adjustments in retailing led to a concentration of activity in larger units.

Notes

1. The nine detailed categories of selected service establishments are as follows. I have added explanatory notes to clarify the kind of services provided by units in each category.

- Hotels, Motels, and Trailering Parks (SIC701, 703). Includes hotels, motor inns, motels, recreational parks, trailering parks.
- Personal Services (SIC72). Includes laundry, cleaning, and other garment services; photographic studios; barber and beauty shops; shoe repair shops; funeral services.
- Business Services (SIC73). Includes advertising, services to dwelling, data processing services, management and consulting services, equipment rental.
- Automotive Repair, Services, and Garages (SIC75). Includes automotive repair, auto leasing and rental, auto parking, auto services.
- Miscellaneous Repair Services (SIC76). Includes electrical and electronic repair, reupholstery and furniture, other repair services.
- Amusement and Recreational Services (SIC78, 79). Includes motion picture theaters; producers, orchestras (except nonprofit), and entertainers; bowling alleys, billiards, pool; other amusement and recreational services.
- Dental Laboratories (SIC8072).
- Legal Services (SIC81).
- Architectural, Engineering, and Land-Surveying Services (SIC891).

Although the list was expanded in 1972 with the inclusion of the legal, dental laboratory, and architectural segments, many services remain outside the scope of the census. Among those functions still excluded are medical, dental, and other professional or scientific services, except for those mentioned above. Other activities not considered include those of educational institutions, religious or charitable organizations, medical centers, public utilities, and government-owned establishments.

2. There have been periodic revisions in the definitions, enumeration procedures, and criteria used by the Census Bureau to collect service data. Such revisions make exact longitudinal comparisons impossible, but do not obscure the general trends in the data, nor preclude comparisons of subgroups within the population. It is difficult to estimate what cumulative impact these revisions have had on the longitudinal compatibility of the data. But it is likely that the reported figures modestly overestimate establishment change and significantly overstate the increase in service expenditures, compared with the figures that would have been obtained had the collection techniques and definitions remained consistent from 1939 to 1972 (Johnson, 1980).

3. There is reason to believe that service sector growth stimulates population gain by creating jobs. However, the selected services examined here employ a small segment of the local labor force and, therefore, have a very limited capacity to generate population shifts through employment change. In addition, these services are heavily dependent on local patronage, with a few exceptions (i.e., hotels and motels). Thus, assigning population change an independent role here does not seriously violate the assumption of a recursive system.

4. Many of the concerns regarding the causal model presented for retailing also apply here. The chances of simultaneity bias may be slightly higher here than in the model for retail trade. But the possibility that such bias seriously affects the model estimates remains low, because the selected services measured by the Bureau of the Census represent a relatively small proportion of the labor force in most nonmetropolitan counties. Thus, incremental shifts in service employment will have only a minimal impact on population change. Procedures similar to those employed for the retail model suggested that multicollinearity is not a concern in this model. In addition, the general structure of the model remained the same when it was examined for shorter time periods.

5
The Recent Revival of Nonmetropolitan Population Growth

Demographic trends in nonmetropolitan areas have shifted dramatically in recent years. The extensive population losses of the first two-thirds of the century reversed in the 1970s. During the 1970s nonmetropolitan areas experienced widespread population increase and migration gains. This remarkable reversal of long-standing demographic trends requires detailed examination because it has significant implications for the business infrastructure serving nonmetropolitan residents.

By now the nonmetropolitan population turnaround is a well documented and widely recognized phenomenon. However, initial reports of the revival of nonmetropolitan population growth were greeted with a great deal of skepticism by the academic community (Wardwell and Brown, 1980). The eventual acceptance of the occurrence of the turnaround is due to the perseverance of a small number of demographers and rural sociologists, many of whom are cited below. This chapter supplements earlier research by adding a historical perspective and by examining the turnaround in a context that makes possible an investigation of how it has influenced the nonmetropolitan business structure in recent years.[1]

Prior Research on the Turnaround

Conventional wisdom holds that economies of scale in agriculture and the long-term shift to an urban economy have operated both to push people out of agricultural and rural areas and to pull them toward metropolitan centers (Beale, 1964). These redistributive pressures drained millions of residents from nonmetropolitan areas between 1920 and 1970, and the resulting rural-to-urban migration stream was among the most stable demographic patterns of U.S. history. Yet recent population data and a growing research literature indicate a remarkable reversal in demographic trends, with nonmetropolitan counties growing more rapidly than their metropolitan counterparts after 1970 (see Beale, 1975; Beale and Fuguitt, 1975; Brown, 1975; Brown and Wardwell, 1980; Zuiches and Brown, 1978; Wardwell and Gilchrist, 1978; Wardwell, 1977). Given the impact that population change has on the commercial infrastructure of an area, a continuation of this turnaround has significant implications for the future development of nonmetropolitan businesses.

A major line of research concerning the turnaround has emphasized the primary role of shifts in migration patterns. Nonmetropolitan areas suffered a net loss of over 6 million people through migration in the 1950s; an additional 3 million left between 1960 and 1970. In contrast, a net inmigration to nonmetropolitan areas of more than 1.6 million persons was reported just between 1970 and 1974 (Beale and Fuguitt, 1976). Such nonmetropolitan migration gains were a function of reduced outmigration as well as increased inmigration. Tucker (1976) estimates that the number of residents leaving nonmetropolitan areas was reduced by 12 percent between 1970 and 1975, while migration into such areas increased by 23 percent.[2]

Natural increase may also be implicated in the nonmetropolitan turnaround. Beale (1969) confirmed the linkage between natural increase and migration in his discussion of the increased incidence of natural decrease among counties with protracted outmigration. Such a linkage is indeed quite provocative, for if a history of outmigration does lead to natural decrease, then the post-1970 migration reversal may also be a factor in natural change.

Research on the linkages between antecedent demographic conditions and the post-1970 trends has always been hindered by the absence of adequate longitudinal data. This chapter uses the grouping of counties based on historical population trends developed in Chapter 2 to provide an appropriate longitudinal context for a review of recent nonmetropolitan demographic trends.[3]

Recent Nonmetropolitan Growth: Departure from Historical Trends

Almost 80 percent of all nonmetropolitan counties gained population between 1970 and 1977, compared to 47 percent between 1960 and 1970. Although this remarkable reversal is now an accepted demographic fact, its pervasiveness, especially among counties with long histories of population decline is not well recognized. The incidence of population gain from 1970 to 1977 was greatest among counties that began growing between 1960 and 1970 after earlier population loss (GAIN6070), but post-1970 gains were only slightly less likely in the other three groups with histories of population increase (Table 5.1). Most counties that grew in earlier years then, continued to grow from 1970 to 1977. Among past losers, post-1970 growth was more likely in counties with shorter histories of population decline. In two of the three groups with past declines of thirty or fewer years, over 70 percent of the counties gained population from 1970 to 1977. Even in the group with consistent population decline of at least forty years' duration, over half the counties grew after 1970. The resurgence of population growth among counties subjected to such prolonged depopulation is the strongest evidence of the pervasiveness of the turnaround.

Another striking contrast to historical trends is evident in the behavior of metropolitan and nonmetropolitan counties. Whereas before 1970 metropolitan status virtually guaranteed population increase, between 1970 and 1977 15.7 percent of all metropolitan counties lost population. And many of these ninety declining metropolitan counties contained a large central city. During the 1970s any nonmetropolitan county with a history of growth of any duration had a greater chance of

TABLE 5.1
Counties with Given History of Population Change 1930 to 1970 by Population Change 1970 to 1977

	LOSS3070	LOSS4070	LOSS5070	LOSS6070	GAIN6070	GAIN5070	GAIN4070	GAIN3070	METRO
Loss GT 7%	9.6%	4.3%	2.4%	3.3%	1.1%	3.5%	0.0%	0.8%	3.7%
Loss LT 7%	36.6	18.8	15.9	26.7	3.6	7.7	7.5	5.1	12.0
Gain LT 7%	37.4	39.1	29.3	39.9	24.3	25.4	36.3	29.1	27.0
Gain GT 7%	16.3	37.8	52.4	30.0	71.0	63.4	56.3	65.0	57.3
Total	99.9%	100.0%	100.0%	99.9%	100.1%	100.0%	100.1%	100.0%	100.0%
	473	373	164	273	441	142	80	474	684

Note: Percentages vary from 100% because of rounding error

gaining population than did a metropolitan county. In fact, even some nonmetropolitan counties with histories of decline before 1970 had nearly as great a chance of gaining population in the 1970s as did a metropolitan county. This phenomenon also represents a significant reversal of long-standing demographic trends.

The magnitude of the reversal may be gauged by comparing recent change to change over the preceding fifty years (Table 5.2). Between 1920 and 1970 the population of nonmetropolitan areas grew by 8.7 million people, an increase of only 19.5 percent. In contrast, the metropolitan population grew by over 87 million, an increase of over 142 percent. Among nonmetropolitan counties, incremental gains between 1920 and 1970 were greatest in the group with the longest history of growth, the 1920 population nearly doubling by 1970. Lesser gains were accumulated by groups with shorter periods of consistent growth, and, as the duration of population decline lengthened, aggregate increases were replaced by losses of increasing proportions.[4]

The pattern of aggregate population change since 1970 contrasts sharply with patterns from the earlier period. Between 1970 and 1977 the nonmetropolitan population grew by 4.9 million, an increase fully 55 percent of that garnered in the preceding fifty years. Aggregate population gains occurred in each of the eight nonmetropolitan county groups between 1970 and 1977. To be sure, these incremental population gains increased as the duration of loss lessened and loss was replaced by growth. However, because each of the four loss cohorts had a net decline in population during the 1960s, the size of the aggregate gains emphasizes the extent of the deviation from past trends. Even more remarkable is the fact that the general nonmetropolitan gain of 9.2 percent was 1.7 times as great as the 5.4 percent metropolitan gain; between 1920 and 1970, the nonmetropolitan gain had been less than 14 percent of the metropolitan gain. Such substantial and widespread growth in counties previously subject to decline or slow growth underscores the significance of the post-1970 turnaround.

TABLE 5.2
Population Change by County Group Between 1920 and 1970 and Change in Population Components 1970 to 1977

| | 1920 - 1970 | | 1970 - 1977 | | | | | |
| | Population Change | | Population Change | | Net Migration | | Natural Increase | |
	Total Change	Percent Change	Total Change	Percent Change	Total Change	Percent Change	Total Change	Percent Change
LOSS3070	-2,641,072	-34.9	78,194	1.6	18,779	0.4	59,415	1.2
LOSS4070	-1,276,415	-19.8	269,250	5.2	110,520	2.1	158,731	3.1
LOSS5070	231,319	7.3	255,833	7.5	109,471	3.2	146,358	4.3
LOSS6070	1,413,318	31.2	286,620	4.8	3,310	0.1	283,310	4.8
GAIN6070	5,342	.1	906,313	12.0	641,963	8.5	264,350	3.5
GAIN5070	522,753	24.1	265,638	9.9	126,873	4.7	138,765	5.2
GAIN4070	734,893	44.7	237,424	10.0	122,697	5.2	114,727	4.8
GAIN3070	9,701,486	84.9	2,588,009	12.3	1,391,996	6.6	1,196,135	5.7
ALL NONMET.	8,691,624	19.5	4,887,281	9.2	2,525,609	4.7	2,361,791	4.4
Metro	87,532,000	142.9	8,031,330	5.4	656,574	0.4	7,377,490	5.0

TABLE 5.3
Change in Population Components Between 1970 and 1977 for Nonmetropolitan County
Groups and Metropolitan Counties

	Population Change		Natural Increase		Net Migration	
	Median Percent Change	% with Pop. Decrease	Median Percent Change	% with Natural Decrease	Median Percent Change	% with Net In- Migration
LOSS3070	0.6	46.2	0.8	39.3	-0.2	49.0
LOSS4070	4.5	23.1	2.7	14.7	1.5	61.4
LOSS5070	7.2	18.3	4.1	3.7	3.0	64.0
LOSS6070	3.1	30.0	4.1	3.3	-0.9	46.2
GAIN6070	11.8	4.7	3.5	11.1	7.9	83.7
GAIN5070	9.5	11.2	4.6	2.8	6.2	82.5
GAIN4070	8.7	7.5	5.4	3.8	3.6	68.7
GAIN3070	10.3	5.9	5.0	3.2	4.7	74.9
All Nonmet	6.3	20.2	3.6	13.6	2.8	65.0
Metro	9.0	15.7	5.5	2.2	3.6	64.5

The Changing Role of Net Migration

Historically, most nonmetropolitan areas consistently lost population to urban centers through migration. When such areas did grow, it was because traditionally high levels of natural increase exceeded the losses from migration. This pattern is exemplified by the 1950s, a decade characterized by extremely heavy migration losses that resulted in widespread population declines despite substantial natural increase (see Chapter 2). During the 1960s net outmigration moderated significantly; the median loss fell to 9 percent, from 17 percent in the 1950s, and inmigration became common among counties with histories of population increase. This moderation proved to be a forerunner of the general trend of the 1970s. Between 1970 and 1977, 65 percent of all nonmetropolitan counties had net inmigration, as against 25 percent with a net inflow from 1960 to 1970 or 12 percent from 1950 to 1960 (see Table 5.3 and Chapter 2). As a result, after decades of very

slow growth the nonmetropolitan population jumped by almost 4.9 million between 1970 and 1977, with nearly half
of the gain coming from net inmigration.

The nonmetropolitan migration gains of the 1970s have
been extremely widespread. The majority of counties in six
of the eight county groups had net inmigration between 1970
and 1977 (Table 5.3). The exceptions are the counties with
the longest histories of population decline (LOSS3070) and
those with the shortest histories of population decline
(LOSS6070), and even in these groups the percentages with
net inmigration are 49 and 46 percent respectively. As Beale
(1975) indicated, substantial inmigration to nonmetropolitan
areas is a significant deviation from traditional demographic
trends. And the widespread incidence of inmigration in previously declining areas, particularly when the loss has been
prolonged, is completely without precedent. This migration
turnaround comes at a time when declining fertility rates are
depriving nonmetropolitan areas of natural increase, their
traditional source of new residents. If previous migration
patterns had continued into the late 1970s, nonmetropolitan
population decline would have been even more widespread
than in preceding decades.

In contrast, less than 10 percent of the metropolitan population increase of the 1970s resulted from migration gains.
Although 65 percent of all metropolitan counties are still
growing through inmigration, the gains are smaller than
historically has been the case. And many of the older, larger
central city counties are now experiencing substantial outmigration. Thus, the rural-to-urban migration stream that
historically fueled the growth of metropolitan areas is no
longer a significant source of population increase for metropolitan areas as a whole. Natural increase is now the primary
source of population increase in metropolitan America.

The Continuing Contribution of Natural Increase

Natural increase has been the primary cause of population
increase in nonmetropolitan areas through most of this century,
but as the previous chapters suggest, its level has fluctuated

through the years. During the 1950s all nonmetropolitan county groups had high rates of natural increase; even among protracted-decline counties the median rate of natural increase was generally above 10 percent. The rate decelerated substantialy during the 1960s, slowing the most among counties with long histories of population decline. This slowdown was largely a function of the temporal decline in fertility associated with the end of the baby boom, but the long years of age-specific outmigration from protracted-decline counties were also beginning to take their toll (Beale, 1969; Chang, 1974; Markides and Tracy, 1977).

The rate of natural increase continued to decline between 1970 and 1977. The nonmetropolitan median fell to an average annual gain of .51 percent between 1970 and 1977, compared with .64 percent between 1965 and 1970 (see Tables 5.2 and 2.6). This slowdown occurred in each of the county groups, with the rate remaining highest among extended-gain counties and lowest in groups with pre-1970 population decline.

The trend in natural increase reflects in large part the continued secular decline in fertility rates. In some areas natural increase was also hindered, as in the 1960s, by an age structure distorted by years of age-selective outmigration. Had it not been for the increased incidence of net inmigration, particularly in LOSS3070 and LOSS4070, the post-1970 period would have been one of punishing population losses rather than population turnaround.

Although most of the excitement surrounding the turnaround has understandably focused on the new migration trends, natural increase is still an important factor in recent nonmetropolitan population gains. The proportion of the total gain attributable to natural increase ranged from a high of 98 percent in LOSS6070 to a low of 29 percent in GAIN6070 (derived from Table 5.2). Natural increase still contributed over half the population gain in five of the eight county groups during the 1970s.

The Rising Incidence of Natural Decrease

As fertility rates declined during the 1970s, natural decrease became more common, affecting 13.6 percent of all nonmetropolitan counties. The counties most likely to suffer natural decrease are those that have been losing population for many years. Almost 40 percent of counties with at least forty years of population loss before 1970 experienced natural decrease between 1970 and 1977. And among counties with thirty years of population loss before 1970, 14.7 percent had more deaths than births between 1970 and 1977. Natural decrease is also evident among counties that began to grow in the 1960s after decades of decline (GAIN6070). It is still quite rare among counties where the onset of population decline has been recent, among counties with histories of population increase, and among metropolitan counties.

Such findings are consistent with previous studies of the demographic aspects of natural decrease, which suggest that a principal cause of such decline is a distorted age structure resulting from the sustained outmigration of young adults from an area (Beale, 1969; Chang, 1974; Markides and Tracy, 1977). In 1970, the median age in nonmetropolitan counties with fifty years of consistent population decline was 34.6 years, compared to 27.9 among counties with fifty years of consistent population increase (Johnson and Purdy, 1980). The combination of few young adults of child-rearing age and a large concentration of older adults with high mortality rates heightens the likelihood of natural decrease, particularly when fertility rates are at a low ebb, as they were during the 1970s.

Clearly the effect of recent inmigration on natural decrease depends on the age makeup of the migration stream, a topic not widely researched. Preliminary evidence indicates that a significant portion of the migration stream is composed of older people who have retired and moved to nonmetropolitan areas (Beale and Fuguitt, 1975). Bowles (1978) found that in migration exchanges between metropolitan and nonmetropolitan areas twice as many persons aged 55 and over left metropolitan areas as moved into them. Nonmetropolitan areas had a net migration gain of 423,000 persons aged 55 and over between 1970 and 1975. To a lesser extent juveniles aged 5–17 were also overrepresented in the migration stream, but Bowles found that the traditional exodus of young adults

(20–24) to the cities is continuing. Zuiches and Brown (1978) report net gains of slightly older adults (25–34) in nonmetropolitan areas, though the actual size of the gain is relatively small. In sum, recent migration has done little to reduce the distortion of local nonmetropolitan age structures. Thus, natural decrease is on the upswing despite recent general nonmetropolitan growth and may become even more common in the future, barring an unforeseen surge in the birth rate.

There may not be enough young women remaining in many protracted-decline counties to produce enough children to offset the deaths of a rapidly aging population. After all, the upturn in births during the early 1980s is more a function of the number of women of child-bearing age than of an increased number of births per woman. Thus, the number of young women in declining counties is a critical factor in any future shifts in natural increase.

The Changing Roles of Migration and Natural Increase

After 1970 the traditional pattern of growth through an excess of natural increase over outmigration occurred in only 20 percent of the nonmetropolitan counties that gained population (Table 5.4). The predominant pattern, characterizing 69 percent of all growing counties, was one of natural increase supplemented by inmigration. This combination was common among counties that grew before 1970; it was less common among counties with histories of consistent population loss of several decades' duration. Although net inmigration coupled with natural decrease was displayed by only 11 percent of all growing counties, it was prominent among counties in long-term loss groups. Counties in this category gained population solely through inmigration; natural change actually exerted a negative effect. Aside from a few cases in the 1960s, this pattern of population growth is unheard of in recent U.S. demographic history. The population increase among metropolitan counties is quite similar to that found among nonmetropolitan gainers, except that natural decrease was much less common.

TABLE 5.4
The Impact of Net Migration and Natural Increase on Overall Population Change in County Groups 1970 to 1977

	Population Gain 1970 - 1977				Population Loss 1970 - 1977			
	Inmigration and Natural Decrease	Outmigration and Natural Increase	Inmigration and Natural Increase	Number of Counties	Outmigration and Natural Decrease	Inmigration and Natural Decrease	Outmigration and Natural Increase	Number of Counties
LOSS3070	33%	20%	47%	(257)	34%	13%	53%	(221)
LOSS4070	13%	21%	66%	(287)	19%	2%	79%	(86)
LOSS5070	3%	22%	75%	(134)	3%	3%	94%	(30)
LOSS6070	4%	35%	62%	(192)	1%	1%	98%	(81)
GAIN6070	11%	13%	76%	(421)	0%	5%	95%	(20)
GAIN5070	3%	18%	79%	(126)	0%	0%	100%	(16)
GAIN4070	4%	26%	70%	(74)	0%	0%	100%	(6)
GAIN3070	3%	21%	76%	(447)	0%	0%	100%	(27)
All Nonmet	11%	20%	69%	(1938)	19%	7%	74%	(487)
Metropolitan	2%	24%	74%	(577)	3%	1%	95%	(107)
All Counties	9%	21%	70%	(2515)	16%	6%	78%	(594)

In contrast, counties that lost population between 1970 and 1977 continued to display the traditional pattern of population decline through an excess of outmigration over natural increase. This pattern occurred in 74 percent of all nonmetropolitan declining counties, and was nearly universal among the relatively few pre-1970 gainers that began to decline after 1970. There also were a few counties, concentrated in the protracted-loss groups, that experienced population decline through the unlikely combination of natural decrease and inmigration. In such counties the minimal migration gains resulting from the turnaround were not sufficient to offset the excess of deaths over births within an aging population. Although rare, this combination represents a signficant deviation from past trends in population change.

An ominous combination affecting 19 percent of all declining nonmetropolitan counties is the joint occurrence of outmigration and natural decrease. Although this figure is smaller than the 24 percent that suffered from this combination between 1970 and 1975, it still represents nearly 100 counties (Johnson and Purdy, 1980). Such counties are heavily concentrated in groups with prolonged histories of population decline, where an age structure already distorted by past migration and low birth rates can no longer sustain natural increase. If this trend continues for any significant length of time, it will not only increase the risk of heavy short-term losses in the affected counties, but also, through continued age-specific migration and a paucity of children, will drain the remaining demographic resilience from them.

In contrast to nonmetropolitan losses, the recent population decline in a signficant number of metropolitan counties is almost purely a function of outmigration. All but 5 of the 107 metropolitan counties that lost population between 1970 and 1977 did so because more people left the county than moved into it.

Growth in Nonmetropolitan Areas: Beyond the Urban Fringe

Many demographers at first suspected that the remarkable population reversal of the 1970s represented the spillover of

metropolitan population into adjacent nonmetropolitan counties (Beale and Fuguitt, 1975). Such a pattern would suggest
continued expansion of the nation's metropolitan centers, with
the apparent turnaround being nothing more than an artifact
of the failure of government definitions to keep up with the
actual limits of metropolitan areas. If this were the case, the
apparently rural gains would represent a continuation of past
trends of deconcentration and peripheral expansion of the
metropolitan population, rather than an entirely new trend
(Hawley, 1971).

The data do indicate that counties adjacent to metropolitan
areas enjoyed substantial population gains after 1970, but
nonadjacent counties also grew significantly. The population
turnaround is thus due to more than urban spillover.

Among nonmetropolitan counties as a group, the sources
of population gain were almost evenly divided between natural
increase and net inmigration. There are significant differences,
however, between counties with and without a large urban
center (Appendix 1). Among counties without a large urban
center, in both adjacent and nonadjacent areas, inmigration
was a more prominent factor in population change than
natural increase. In contrast, natural increase was a more
significant influence among counties with a large urban place,
particularly if they were not adjacent to a metropolitan center.
Beale (1975) has suggested that this difference is due to an
age structure more conducive to natural increase in counties
with a large urban place, especially nonadjacent ones.

To clarify the impact of adjacency and size of largest place
on the likelihood of post-1970 growth, I introduced them as
controls on four groups of counties categorized according to
pre-1970 population change (see Appendix). Size of largest
place exerted a modest influence on the likelihood of recent
growth. Among these groups post-1970 gains were more likely
among counties without a large urban place, because such
counties had higher rates of inmigration. Lower inmigration
was partially offset by greater natural increase in counties
with a large urban place. Aside from a minor impact on
protracted-loss cohorts, adjacency did little to differentiate
post-1970 gainers from losers. The limited utility of size of

place and adjacency as controls underscores the pervasive character of the post-1970 reversal.

Population increase, inmigration, and natural increase occurred between 1970 and 1977 in virtually every category of counties classified by history of population change, adjacency, and size of largest place. Only among the nine counties with a history of population decline that included a large urban place and were not adjacent to a metropolitan area was there an aggregate population decline as a result of migration losses. Every other subcategory of counties enjoyed an aggregate gain of population through both natural increase and net migration. This phenomenon is not a function of spectacular gains in a few counties overshadowing losses in many; in virtually every subcategory, the majority of counties experienced population increase, net inmigration, and natural increase between 1970 and 1977. The only exceptions are among nonadjacent counties with long histories of population decline and among adjacent counties with a short history of population loss that contain a large urban place.

Conclusion

The recent reversal of long-standing nonmetropolitan population trends has been pervasive, affecting counties with a variety of histories of growth and decline over the preceding forty years. Although post-1970 population gain was most likely among counties that have grown historically, of those counties subjected to consistent population decline for as long as forty years a majority have also started to grow again.

An important factor in this turnaround is the widespread occurrence of net inmigration in nonmetropolitan counties, a rare event in the earlier decades of this century. This net inmigration comes at a time when levels of natural increase are very low, not only because of shifts in fertility behavior among couples but also because of the impact of past outmigration on the age structure of many nonmetropolitan areas. In recent years the incidence of natural decrease, virtually nonexistent in earlier times, has increased dramatically, particularly among counties with long histories of population decline. The pattern of significant inmigration coupled with low levels of natural increase represents a clear break with the past pattern of nonmetropolitan growth through an excess of natural increase over outmigration.

Finally, the evidence substantiates earlier claims that the revival of growth in nonmetropolitan areas is more than an artifact of urban spillover. In many cases the fastest growing counties have been those remote from metropolitan areas and without any large urban place. Much of the impetus for this growth has come from inmigration, though natural increase is still important. If this nonmetropolitan renaissance persists, it will end a rural-to-urban population shift that has spanned most of U.S. history.

Notes

1. In order to facilitate comparisons with business data from the 1977 Economic Census (the latest currently available), I have used demographic data spanning only the period from 1970 to 1977. This limitation makes the demographic analysis here somewhat dated; however, using more recent demographic data seriously complicates comparisons with the older economic data, because infrastructure shifts lag behind population change. Thus, because the linkage between population change and business changes is the primary focus of this study, I have reluctantly opted for the older demographic data. In any case, the basic findings reported here regarding the pervasiveness of the nonmetropolitan turnaround would be the same if more recent demographic data were used.

2. I shall not here discuss the causes of the nonmetropolitan population turnaround. Demographers still do not fully understand the factors underlying it, and even a brief review of their findings to date would require more space than is available. In any event, such a review is beyond the purview of this study, whose main concern is the consequences of population change, not its causes. For those interested in the causes of the turnaround, a good overview with references to most of the important literature is available in Wardwell and Brown (1980).

3. One must exercise caution in interpreting the demographic data for the period from 1970 to 1977. The population of a county

and net migration to or from it are Bureau of the Census estimates, whereas the reported births and deaths are derived from *Vital Statistics* (Bureau of the Census, 1980). Thus, the actual population and rate of net migration for a specific county might vary from the estimates used here. However, the variations are likely to be minor, and there is little doubt that the general patterns derived from such data are quite similar to the actual national trends. In addition, the turnaround as a whole has been documented from a variety of data sources (Tucker, 1976; Brown and Wardwell, 1980).

4. The peculiar ranking of LOSS6070 and GAIN6070 in Table 5.2 stems from the abbreviated period of consistent change in these groups. Many counties in the former category grew for decades before declining between 1960 and 1970; hence the large 1920–1970 population gain. The counties in the latter category were more heterogeneous, with mixed histories of loss and gain.

6
The Impact of the Population Turnaround on Nonmetropolitan Business

The widespread resurgence of population increase in non-metropolitan areas has significant implications for the local business infrastructure. Historical evidence suggests that business expansion should follow in the wake of the turnaround, but that the local business infrastructure will not fully reflect population change for some time. There is already evidence that the turnaround is stimulating a business renaissance: during the middle 1970s nonmetropolitan business growth rates exceeded those in metropolitan areas, a pattern without precedent in recent times. The 1977 Economic Census is the latest currently available, and the first portions of this chapter are consequently limited to the early years of the turnaround. The last section of the chapter reviews sample data for 1977–1982.

The Turnaround and Retailing

The counties with the greatest sales gains between 1972 and 1977 were those distant from the metropolitan centers that have historically dominated retailing. Such nonadjacent nonmetropolitan counties were the only ones with accelerated retail spending in the middle 1970s. The retail acceleration in such counties was modest, rising from 13 percent over 1967–1972 to 13.8 percent over 1972–1977, but it contrasts sharply with the pattern among adjacent and metropolitan counties (Table 6.1). Retail sales gains in metropolitan counties in the middle 1970s slowed to less than half of what they had been in the preceding five years. Even among the faster growing adjacent nonmetropolitan counties, sales gains in the middle 1970s were smaller than in the earlier part of the decade.

Such rapid retail growth in nonmetropolitan areas represents a fundamental break with historical trends. Traditionally, retail growth has been most rapid in metropolitan areas and slowest in rural areas far from the urban centers. For example, between 1930 and 1967, retail trade in areas that would by 1974 be defined as metropolitan increased 231 percent after adjustment for inflation. Nonmetropolitan sales increased by only 180 percent during the same period.

Nonmetropolitan retail sales data for 1967–1972 still reflected this traditional pattern. The largest gains occurred in metropolitan counties, followed by nonmetropolitan counties adjacent to metropolitan areas. Retail gains were smallest in nonmetropolitan counties distant from urban areas. During the 1970s, however, the pattern of retail growth reversed itself. Retail expenditures in metropolitan areas, corrected for inflation, increased by only 7.4 percent between 1972 and 1977—a dramatic slowdown from the 19 percent gain between 1967 and 1972. Adjacent nonmetropolitan counties also experienced less retail growth in the middle 1970s, though the slowdown was much less drastic. Only among the remote counties did retail spending actually accelerate in the middle 1970s.

The retailing renaissance is not limited to a single geographical region. During the 1970s, nonmetropolitan retail gains exceeded those in urban areas in thirty of the forty-six states containing a metropolitan center (Figure 6.1). States where metropolitan gains continued to be greater either were in the booming sunbelt, or contained only one or two small metropolitan areas.

TABLE 6.1
Population and Retail Sales for 1977 and Aggregate Percentage Change in Population and Sales from 1967 to 1972
and 1972 to 1977 based on Metropolitan Status and Adjacency

	# of Counties	1977		1967 to 1972		1972 to 1977	
		Total Population	Total Sales	Population Change	Sales Change	Population Change	Sales Change
Nonmetro-Nonadjacent	1,470	27.8	83.6	3.2%	13.0%	5.5%	13.8%
Nonmetro-Adjacent	955	30.2	85.7	5.7%	15.0%	6.1%	12.0%
Metropolitan	643	156.3	537.5	6.3%	19.4%	3.2%	7.4%
All Counties	3,068	212.2	706.8	5.8%	18.1%	3.9%	8.4%

Note: Population in millions as of 1977
Sales in billions of 1977 dollars, includes sales tax and finance charges before 1977
Percentage increase in sales is corrected for inflation
Metro status as of 1974

120

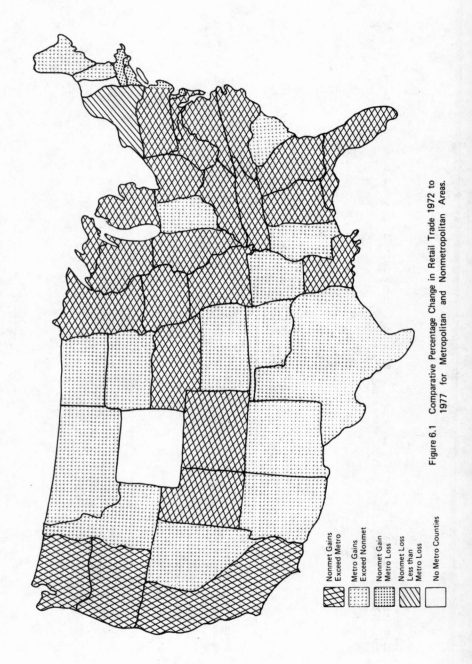

Figure 6.1 Comparative Percentage Change in Retail Trade 1972 to 1977 for Metropolitan and Nonmetropolitan Areas.

Nonmet Gains
Exceed Metro

Metro Gains
Exceed Nonmet

Nonmet Gain
Metro Loss

Nonmet Loss
Less than
Metro Loss

No Metro Counties

What Caused the Rural Retail Renaissance?

The widespread population increase in nonmetropolitan areas during the 1970s was a major cause of the rural retailing boom. The nature and extent of this remarkable population turnaround have already been considered, but several points pertinent to retail trends bear repeating. Between 1970 and 1977, 80 percent of the nation's nonmetropolitan counties gained population—more than at any other time in this century. Nonmetropolitan areas gained nearly 5 million people between 1970 and 1977, a significant number of them in-migrants from urban areas. Such inmigration has implications beyond mere increase in population, because urban dwellers who move to nonmetropolitan areas retain their urban consumer tastes and demand a wider variety of goods and services from local businesses.

To appreciate the significance of this population turnaround, recall that between 1930 and 1970 the nonmetropolitan population grew by only 8 million, while metropolitan areas gained over 80 million residents. As a result, the proportion of all retailing done in nonmetropolitan areas declined before leveling off at about 24 percent of the country's total retail sales (Figure 6.2).

Regrouping counties according to their histories of population change provides compelling evidence of the impact such population shifts have had on retailing. For the purposes of this chapter, I have divided metropolitan counties simply into those that were growing in the 1970s and those that were declining, and nonmetropolitan counties into four groups according to their growth behavior before and after 1970. Nonmetropolitan Continuing Gain includes all those counties in GAIN3070, GAIN4070, GAIN5070, and GAIN6070 that continued to gain population during the 1970s; Nonmetropolitan Turnaround Loss comprises those counties in the same four groups that began to lose population in the 1970s. Nonmetropolitan Continuing Loss includes all those counties in LOSS3070, LOSS4070, LOSS5070, and LOSS6070 that continued to lose population during the seventies; Nonme-

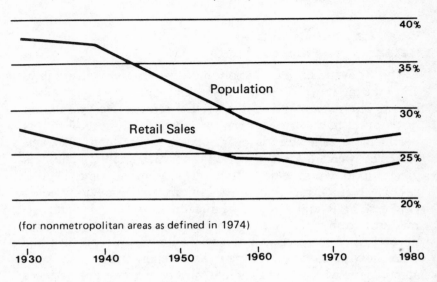

40%

35%

Population

30%

Retail Sales

25%

20%

(for nonmetropolitan areas as defined in 1974)

1930   1940   1950   1960   1970   1980

Figure 6.2   Percentage of Total U.S. Population and Retail Sales
              In Nonmetropolitan Areas of the U.S. 1930 - 1977

tropolitan Turnaround Gain comprises those counties where
population change reversed from loss to gain.

Nonmetropolitan retail gains during the middle seventies
were greatest in the 1066 counties that were gaining both
before and after 1970 (Table 6.2). Many of the counties in
this group have gained population consistently for several
decades. And, as earlier chapters showed, counties with
protracted population increase have consistently had the highest rates of retail increase. By the middle 1970s, retail gains
in such counties rivaled those of the fastest growing metropolitan counties. These retail gains were fueled by the high
and sustained population increase such counties experienced
between 1967 and 1977. In fact, by the middle 1970s, the
population growth rate in this group exceeded that of the
growing metropolitan counties. Counties in this growing
nonmetropolitan group were larger than other nonmetropolitan counties. On the average they contained 33,000 residents and had retail spending of more than 102 million

TABLE 6.2
Mean Population and Retail Sales in 1977 and Aggregate Percentage Change in Population and Sales from 1967 to 1972 and 1972 to 1977 for Counties Grouped by Comparing Historical Population Trends to Those Between 1970 and 1977

	# of Counties	1977		1967 to 1972		1972 to 1977	
		Mean Population	Mean Sales	Population Change	Sales Change	Population Change	Sales Change
Nonmetro Loss	419	12,182	$ 31.7	-3.7%	9.9%	-2.7%	4.1%
Nonmetro Turnaround Gain	869	17,531	46.4	.4%	9.0%	4.8%	12.7%
Nonmetro Turnaround Loss	71	32,037	101.0	2.3%	7.3%	-3.6%	6.1%
Nonmetro Gain	1,066	33,252	102.3	8.1%	20.7%	8.3%	14.3%
Metro Declining	90	640,635	2,139.4	-.3%	6.1%	-4.1%	-3.7%
Metro Growing	553	174,789	623.8	11.2%	30.3%	7.4%	15.0%
All Counties	3,068	69,223	$ 230.9	5.8%	18.1%	3.9%	8.4%

Note: Sales in millions of 1977 dollars, includes sales tax and finance charges before 1977
Percentage change in sales is corrected for inflation
Metro status as of 1974

dollars in 1977. Many include a large town serving as the principal shopping center for a multicounty region. Thus, they have a customer base large enough to support all but the most specialized retail functions.

The turnaround's impact on retailing is reflected most clearly among the 869 nonmetropolitan counties that gained population during the 1970s after declining in previous decades (Nonmetro Turnaround Gain). Such counties had a 4.8 percent increase in population during the middle 1970s, compared to a gain of only .4 percent between 1967 and 1972, when the population turnaround was beginning. Counties undergoing such a turnaround were the only ones with greater retail sales gains in the middle 1970s than in the previous five years. Between 1967 and 1972, retail sales grew by only 9 percent in such counties, a rate of increase only half as great as that for the nation as a whole. In contrast, these turnaround counties experienced a 12.7 percent increase in retail sales between 1972 and 1977, a rate fully 50 percent above the national average. In fact, the rate of retail increase in these counties between 1972 and 1977 was only slightly less than among the fastest growing counties. Counties that shifted from decline to growth have fewer residents and lower retail sales than their nonmetropolitan counterparts with continuous growth. They also are less likely to include a large town and more likely to be remote from a metropolitan area. However, most are growing through inmigration, with much of it coming from metropolitan areas, making it likely that the growing numbers of residents also have rising consumer expectations.

Excitement about the population turnaround often overshadows the fact that 419 nonmetropolitan counties continued to lose population through the 1970s (Nonmetropolitan Continuing Loss). Many have been losing residents for decades, and though the turnaround reduced the loss in many of them, it has not reversed it. Retail sales gains in such counties were minimal between 1972 and 1977. The aggregate retail gain was only 4.1 percent and was largely a function of rising incomes. Declining counties had smaller populations and retail revenues than turnaround gain counties, but in other ways were quite similar to them. The impact of continuing population losses is clearly reflected in the contrast between the rapid retail gains in turnaround gain counties and the very slow growth among continuing-decline counties.

Seventy-one nonmetropolitan counties began to lose population in the 1970s after growing in the previous decade (Nonmetro Turnaround Loss). The trend in such counties is in sharp contrast to that in most nonmetropolitan areas. Counties in this group were quite large, averaging 32,000 residents and over 100 million dollars in retail sales in 1977. Although such counties were still growing in the late 1960s, in retrospect it is evident that they were growing much more slowly than their counterparts that continued to grow in the 1970s. Again, the impact of population loss is reflected in the fact that the aggregate retail gain in this group was only 6.1 percent, compared to 14.3 percent among counties with continued growth in the 1970s.

The greatest retail gains and largest concentration of buying power were in the 553 metropolitan counties that continued to gain population after 1970. Between 1972 and 1977, they gained 6.2 million residents and over 45 billion dollars in retail sales. Most of these counties were in smaller SMSAs, or on the outer suburban fringe of large metropolitan areas.

Metropolitan retail growth in general slowed because ninety urban counties lost population. Their combined loss exceeded 2.5 million residents between 1972 and 1977. As a result, real dollar retail spending in such areas declined by 7 billion dollars. To be sure, inflation pushed current dollar sales higher in most of these counties, but at a slower rate than elsewhere. Many of the nation's largest cities were in such counties, including New York, Chicago, Cleveland, Milwaukee, St. Louis, San Francisco, and Philadelphia.

The dismal retail record and declining population in such areas did not totally discourage commercial expansion. Often retailing thrived in the suburbs, but declined in the central city. Chicago is a case in point. Inflation-corrected retail sales declined 17.5 percent in the city between 1972 and 1977, but grew by 15 percent in the remainder of Cook County.

Generally, growing metropolitan counties registered the greatest sales gains in virtually every type of retailing. But nonmetropolitan counties with continuing population increase were close behind. In fact, the two groups of counties had similar growth rates for food, automotive, hardware, and apparel sales. In contrast, in declining metropolitan markets almost every type of retailing stagnated; general merchandising, furniture, drugs, and apparel were particularly hard hit.

Several factors other than population stimulated increased retail activity in nonmetropolitan areas. Many of these factors were discussed in previous chapters, but bear repeating. Nonmetropolitan incomes, and with them the buying power of nonmetropolitan residents, rose more rapidly than those in urban areas during the seventies. Though nonmetropolitan families still earned less, the gap was now much narrower. In 1930, a nonmetropolitan shopper spent 61 cents for every dollar spent by a metropolitan contemporary. By 1977, the rural shopper spent 83 cents to every urban dollar.

The shift away from agriculture, accompanied by rising educational levels in nonmetropolitan areas, also changed nonmetropolitan buying patterns. The increasingly influential mass media have encouraged nonmetropolitan residents to spend in patterns more like those of their metropolitan counterparts. The once substantial time lag between the acceptance of a new product or innovation in the city and its acceptance in the country no longer exists.

Nonmetropolitan residents are now more willing to travel to reach good shopping facilities. Improvements in the transportation system, such as the interstate highways, have made it easier for nonmetropolitan residents to travel significant distances for shopping. Trips of forty miles to a major retail center are now common. The fact that nonmetropolitan retail centers draw customers from much larger geographic areas than do urban retail districts offsets lower population density. Even high-volume, general merchandise stores can find an adequate customer base today in areas that would not have looked so promising a decade ago. Traditionally, such large retailers depended on high metropolitan population densities to provide their customer base. However, as metropolitan markets approach saturation and retail planners appreciate the opportunities available in nonmetropolitan areas, things are changing.

The final factor that has stimulated recent rises in nonmetropolitan retailing is the growing interest in rural retailing among major firms. As the *Wall Street Journal* reported in 1981, "Big-time retailing is looking increasingly to small-town America for growth." Many general merchandisers did not originally consider even the "middle markets" of small metropolitan areas large enough to support the chain department stores that anchor all major retail centers. However, as opportunities for growth in large metropolitan markets diminished, smaller cities became prime areas for expansion. Now even such general merchandisers as Sears, K-Mart, and J. C. Penney have expanded into the middle markets. To operate efficiently in small metropolitan markets, the chains developed smaller versions of their standard stores. These units have less floor space and significantly smaller staffs than their big-city counterparts, but they carry nearly a full line of merchandise. They meet the demands of an increasingly affluent and style-conscious clientele—and produce adequate profits. Now, retailers are taking the next step, starting to pay selected nonmetropolitan markets the attention they deserve, based on their increased population and purchasing power.

Most fast-food and convenience chains have operated in nonmetropolitan areas for some time. Their outlets, which require relatively small customer bases, are ideally suited for the hundreds of small cities and towns scattered through the nonmetropolitan regions of the country. Now the general merchandisers are joining them. The units they have opened so far are similar to those in the burgeoning middle markets—smaller than those in large metropolitan markets, but offering nearly a full line of merchandise.

Some retail firms concentrate almost exclusively on nonmetropolitan markets, and have been in the best position to take advantage of growth there. Among them is Wal-Mart, a well-regarded general merchandise chain in the middle South. Most of its 330 stores are in nonmetropolitan towns of less than 20,000. Often a Wal-Mart unit is the largest nonfood retailer in town. An average Wal-Mart store generates sales of 4.5 million dollars, and the firm has a projected annual growth rate of 20 percent through 1986. Wal-Mart's example indicates the opportunities for an even higher volume of retailing in nonmetropolitan markets.

One reason some retailers have ignored rural opportunities is that planners accustomed to the smaller zones of demand in urban areas have underestimated the potential of non-metropolitan sites by failing to consider the larger geographical area a single retailing center covers. Recently, however, market development staffs have come to appreciate the greater demand radii common in nonmetropolitan markets.

The Impact of Demand Shifts on the Retail Infrastructure

Because detailed business data are available only through 1977, no detailed model can yet be developed for the impact of population change on the retail structure. As the previous chapters suggest, it often takes decades for the local business infrastructure to adjust fully to significant population and retail spending shifts. Nonetheless, some preliminary guesses can be made about how the infrastructure is responding to recent population trends.

The data for 1972 to 1977 show that the reversal of the traditional pattern of retail sales growth rates stimulated by the turnaround has already started to influence the retail infrastructure. During the 1970s, retail employment and the number of retail units experienced a reversal similar to that in retail spending. Gains were greatest (or losses smallest) in nonadjacent nonmetropolitan areas; gains were smallest (or losses greatest) in metropolitan counties. For example, the number of retail units declined by only 2.4 percent among nonmetropolitan counties, but by more than 3.5 percent in metropolitan areas (Table 6.3). Retail employees increased by 20.9 percent in nonmetropolitan nonadjacent counties between 1972 and 1977, but by only slightly over 10 percent in metropolitan counties. This pattern of change in both establishments and employment is consistent with that for population and retail sales during the middle 1970s, but contrasts with historical patterns of change, including those for 1967 to 1972.[1]

TABLE 6.3
Mean Retail Employment and Establishments 1977 and Aggregate Precentage Change in Employment and Establishments from 1967 to 1972 and 1972 to 1977 by Metropolitan Status and Adjacency

	# of Counties	1977		1967 to 1972		1972 to 1977	
		Total # of Units	Total # of Employees	Unit Change	Employee Change	Unit Change	Employee Change
Nonmetro-Nonadjacent	1,470	299	1,694	3.6%	7.2%	-2.4%	20.9%
Nonmetro-Adjacent	955	294	1,700	5.1%	10.0%	-2.4%	18.0%
Metropolitan	643	1,229	10,648	11.4%	15.0%	-3.5%	11.7%
All Counties	3,068	1,822	14,042	10.0%	13.5%	-3.2%	13.5%

Note: Number of units and employees reported in thousands
Metro status as of 1974

Grouping counties according to population trends further illustrates the strong positive link between population shifts and the retail infrastructure. Only the two county groups with continuing population increases managed to gain retail units during the middle 1970s. The establishment gain of .8 percent in growing metropolitan counties was roughly equivalent to the gain of .5 percent in continuing-growth nonmetropolitan counties (Table 6.4). Counties in these two groups also have the greatest employment increases.

The strong positive association between population change and the retail infrastructure is also evident in the behavior of counties that declined in the 1960s but grew in the 1970s. Such turnaround gain counties suffered establishment losses and stagnant employment levels during the late 1960s, at a time when establishment and employment gains were the rule. Although these counties still lost a modest number of establishments during the 1970s, they experienced a substantial employment gain of 18.5 percent. Their significant increase in retail sales, fueled in large part by population gains, helped moderate the loss of units and accelerate local employment gains.

The negative impact of population decline on the retail infrastructure is evident in data for the three county groups that lost population during the 1970s. Unit losses were greatest (−10.7 percent) among nonmetropolitan counties with sustained population decline. Surprisingly, even though the number of units declined sharply, retail employment still increased by more than 11 percent among such counties. Thus, the historical pattern of an increasing concentration of retail activity in fewer, larger units continued here as it did among most other county groups. Heavy unit losses also occurred in declining metropolitan counties, which suffered a net loss of sales during the middle 1970s. Sales and establishment losses together affected employment; among such counties the retail labor force grew only slightly (1.6 percent), whereas significant employment gains were common in each of the seven other county groups. Finally, in turnaround loss counties population decline reduced retail sales gains, causing the

TABLE 6.4
Mean Retail Employment and Establishments 1977 and Aggregate Percentage Change in Employment and Establishments from 1967 to 1972 and 1972 to 1977 for Counties Grouped by Comparing Historical Population Trends to Those Between 1970 and 1977

	# of Counties	1977		1967 to 1972		1972 to 1977	
		Mean # of Units	Mean # Employees	Unit Change	Employee Change	Unit Change	Employee Change
Nonmetro Loss	419	136	684	-6.4%	-8.5%	-10.7%	11.3%
Nonmetro Turnaround Gain	869	179	921	-1.1%	.9%	- 4.8%	18.5%
Nonmetro Turnaround Loss	71	316	2,083	3.6%	8.4%	- 7.3%	8.8%
Nonmetro Gain	1,066	335	2,027	9.4%	15.1%	.5%	21.5%
Metro Declining	90	4,944	43,562	na	na	-10.3%	1.6%
Metro Growing	553	1,418	12,159	na	na	.8%	22.0%
All Counties	3,068	594	4,603	10.0%	13.5%	- 3.2%	13.5%

Note: Metro status as of 1974
Metropolitan employment change 1972 to 1977 estimated using paid employees
na = Data not available in database used

number of retail units to decline and the number of employees to grow relatively slowly.

Evidently, the nonmetropolitan population turnaround has stimulated increased retail spending in most areas. The resulting infrastructure changes are similar to the historical patterns analyzed in earlier chapters. That is, population gain has stimulated infrastructure expansion (or minimized losses), while population decline has exacerbated losses (or reduced gains).

The Population Turnaround
and the Service Sector

As Chapter 4 explains, population change has historically had less impact on the service sector than on retailing, because other factors (including lifestyle changes, the increasing complexity of equipment, and the proliferation of new services) have stimulated the demand for services. Also, service spending is much more concentrated in metropolitan areas than retail spending. The receipts trends in the selected services considered here do indicate, however, that the population turnaround significantly influenced the nonmetropolitan demand for services. Nonmetropolitan counties that were not adjacent to an SMSA had the greatest gains in receipts during the 1970s. The aggregate gain in such counties was more than 18 percent, nearly twice as large as that for the nation as a whole (Table 6.5). Gains among adjacent nonmetropolitan counties also exceeded those for the nation as a whole. The increase in receipts was smallest among metropolitan counties, which registered an aggregate gain of only 8.7 percent, less than that for the nation as a whole—a sharp departure from historical trends, which have consistently shown metropolitan gains exceeding nonmetropolitan gains by a substantial margin.[2]

A closer look at trends in service receipts among counties grouped according to their pattern of population change further illustrates the impact the nonmetropolitan population turnaround had on these selected services. County groups

TABLE 6.5
Population and Service Receipts for 1977 and Aggregate Percentage Changes in Population and Receipts from 1967 to 1972 and from 1970 to 1977 by Metropolitan Status and Adjacency

	# of Counties	1977		1967 to 1972		1972 to 1977	
		Total Population	Total Receipts	Population Change	Receipts Change	Population Change	Receipts Change
Nonmetro-Nonadjacent	1470	27.8	11.7	3.2%	46.0%	5.5%	18.3%
Nonmetro-Adjacent	955	30.2	11.0	5.7%	46.2%	6.1%	15.2%
Metropolitan	643	156.3	151.4	6.3%	48.2%	3.2%	8.7%
All Counties	3068	212.2	174.1	5.8%	47.9%	3.9%	9.7%

Note: Population in millions as of 1977
Receipts in billions of 1977 dollars, includes sales tax and finance charges before 1977
Percentage increase in sales is corrected for inflation
Metro Status as of 1974

that lost population during the 1970s all had much smaller increases in receipts than those that gained population. In fact, metropolitan counties that lost population suffered a 4.4 percent loss in inflation-corrected service spending between 1972 and 1977 (Table 6.6). The occurrence of such a loss in the fast-growing service sector is rare historically, and the fact that it coincided with a similar retail loss among such counties during the same period suggests that factors were operating in them to discourage spending. Their loss of over 2.5 million residents undoubtedly contributed to their retail and service losses, especially as many of those leaving were middle- and upper-income families who spend heavily on retailing and services.

The two groups of nonmetropolitan counties that lost population during the 1970s did not experience a service receipts decline like that among declining metropolitan counties, perhaps in part because their losses were smaller and in part because those leaving were not as disproportionately middle- and upper-income people. Still, the 4.9 percent gain in receipts among counties with continued population loss and the 8.6 percent gain among turnaround loss counties lagged far behind the gains in counties with growing populations. This difference confirms that population change is exerting a significant causal influence on the business infrastructure.

Growing metropolitan counties traditionally have had the most rapidly growing service sectors, and this pattern continued into the 1970s. The gain of 24.4 percent registered among such counties during the 1970s exceeds the receipts gain of any other county group by a substantial margin. Service receipts gains were also large among nonmetropolitan counties that continued to gain population during the 1970s. The service sector in this county group has traditionally expanded quite consistently, though its infrastructure remains much smaller than that found in metropolitan counties. For example, service receipts in the average nonmetropolitan growing county were only 14.8 million dollars in 1977, compared to 143.3 million among metropolitan growing counties, despite the former's larger population increase, (Table

TABLE 6.6
Mean Population and Service Receipts in 1977 and Aggregate Percentage Change in Population and Receipts from 1967 to 1972 and 1972 to 1977 for Counties Grouped by Comparing Historical Population Trends to Those Between 1970 and 1977

	# of Counties	1977 Mean Population	1977 Mean Receipts	1967 to 1972 Population Change	1967 to 1972 Receipts Change	1972 to 1977 Population Change	1972 to 1977 Receipts Change
Nonmetro Loss	419	12,182	3.6	-3.7%	28.8%	-2.7%	4.9%
Nonmetro Turnaround Gain	869	17,531	5.3	.4%	40.4%	4.8%	13.1%
Nonmetro Turnaround Loss	71	32,037	13.2	2.3%	41.1%	-3.6%	8.6%
Nonmetro Gain	1,066	33,252	14.8	8.1%	50.5%	8.3%	19.8%
Metro Declining	90	640,635	805.2	-.3%	32.9%	-4.1%	-4.4%
Metro Growing	553	174,789	143.3	11.2%	71.7%	7.4%	24.4%
All Counties	3,068	69,223	57.2	5.8%	47.9%	3.9%	9.7%

Note: Receipts in millions of 1977 dollars; includes sales tax and finance charges before 1977
Percentage change in sales is corrected for inflation
Metro status as of 1974

6.6). In part this difference is a function of the larger actual population in the latter group of counties, but it also reflects the concentration of service activity in the nation's urban centers. These data also show that factors other than population change also exerted an influence on service receipts. Note that growing metropolitan counties enjoyed a larger sales increment than nonmetropolitan counties with consistent population increase, despite the latter's larger population increase.

Among counties that shifted from population decline in the late 1960s to population gain in the middle 1970s, the aggregate service receipts gain was 13.1 percent, a figure well above the national gain of 9.7 percent. These same counties had had a gain less than that for the nation as a whole between 1967 and 1972.

In sum, the relationship between population shifts and changes in the volume of service receipts during the 1970s was similar to that reported for retailing. That is, service spending gains were greatest among continuing-growth counties and smallest (or, in the case of declining metropolitan counties, nonexistent) among counties that lost population. Counties that turned around from population loss to gain or from gain to loss had intermediate service receipts gains.

The close association between the pattern of population change and service receipts during the 1970s is rather surprising in view of the historically modest linkage between the two. The pattern between 1967 and 1972 more closely reflects historical trends: county groups with greater population increase had larger gains in receipts, while those with population losses lagged behind. However, even among the nonmetropolitan group that suffered a 3.7 percent decline in population between 1967 and 1972, expenditures on services still grew substantially, because a variety of factors in addition to population change influence the service sector. It is too early yet to tell whether the trend of the 1970s reflects a major change in the service sector. Certainly, the decline in service spending in metropolitan counties that lost population is unusual, as are the rather slow gains among several other groups. It is possible that in times of economic distress the factors that have historically fueled rapid service sector expansion are not as strong. Thus, the influence of population change becomes more significant. As data for the 1980s become available, it will be possible to clarify the linkage between population change and the demand for services.

Recent Population Trends and the Service Infrastructure

The historically rapid expansion of the service infrastructure slowed during the 1970s, probably as a result of the slower increase in demand for services fostered by the difficult economic times. However, there is a curious lack of relationship between population change and change in the service infrastructure when counties are grouped according to metropolitan status and adjacency. This apparent lack of relationship is surprising in view of the strong influence population change had on service receipts during the 1970s. The largest aggregate establishment gain (15.8 percent) was among metropolitan counties, even though they had the smallest population and receipts gains (Table 6.7). In contrast, the smallest unit gain was among nonadjacent nonmetropolitan counties, despite large population and receipts gains. There is a similar lack of relationship between population and employment change when counties are grouped in this manner.

This apparent lack of relationship is explained when counties are grouped according to their history of population change. Such a grouping demonstrates an association between the population shifts fostered by the rural turnaround and changes in the number of service employees and establishments. In this instance, grouping counties by adjacency and metropolitan status obscures the impact of population change by clustering growing and declining counties together.

The service infrastructure expanded most rapidly in the two county groups with histories of population increase that continued to grow during the 1970s (Table 6.8). Metropolitan counties that gained population had the greatest establishment and employment gains, as in retailing. Infrastructure gains were nearly as great among nonmetropolitan continuing-growth counties.

TABLE 6.7
Service Employment and Establishments in 1977 and Aggregate Percentage Change in Employment and Establishments from 1967 to 1972 and 1972 to 1977 by Metropolitan Status and Adjacency

	1977			1967 to 1972		1972 to 1977	
	# of Counties	Total # of Units	Total # of Employees	Unit Change	Employee Change	Unit Change	Employee Change
Nonmetro-Nonadjacent	1,470	227	660	21.5%	40.3%	12.8%	22.4%
Nonmetro-Adjacent	955	229	623	23.0%	39.4%	14.6%	20.3%
Metropolitan	643	1,340	6,501	37.4%	35.1%	15.8%	20.1%
All Counties	3,068	1,797	7,784	33.2%	35.7%	15.3%	20.3%

Note: Number of units and employees reported in thousands
Employment change 1967 to 1972 estimated using paid employment change
Metro status as of 1974

TABLE 6.8
Mean Service Employment and Establishments in 1977 and Aggregate Percentage Change in Employment and Establishments from 1967 to 1972 and 1972 to 1977 for Counties Grouped by Comparing Historical Population Trends to Those Between 1970 and 1977

	# of Counties	1977		1967 to 1972		1972 to 1977	
		Mean # of Units	Mean # of Employees	Unit Change	Employee Change	Unit Change	Employee Change
Nonmetro Loss	419	98	241	11.1%	22.0%	3.8%	15.1%
Nonmetro Turnaround Gain	869	126	320	17.6%	32.1%	8.9%	16.5%
Nonmetro Turnaround Loss	71	254	781	17.9%	36.0%	8.0%	16.7%
Nonmetro Gain	1,066	269	808	26.5%	45.0%	17.6%	24.3%
Metro Declining	90	5,750	31,814	na	na	6.6%	9.8%
Metro Growing	553	1,487	6,638	na	na	22.5%	29.6%
All Counties	3,068	586	2,609	33.2%	35.7%	15.3%	20.3%

Note: Metro status as of 1974
Employment change 1967 to 1972 estimated using change in paid employment
na = Data not available in database

A lag between the onset of population increase and service infrastructure shifts is evident among nonmetropolitan turnaround gain counties. Such counties experienced a moderately large population and receipts gain during the middle 1970s, but had much more modest employment and unit gains. Nonmetropolitan turnaround loss counties had relatively small gains in receipts, but continued to have modest employment and establishment gains. Together, these two patterns suggest that inertia is an important factor in infrastructure change, and that it will be some time before the impact of recent population shifts is fully reflected in the service infrastructure of the affected counties.

Employment and establishment gains were smallest among nonmetropolitan counties that continued to lose population during the 1970s, as well as among metropolitan counties that lost population. However, even among the metropolitan counties where population loss caused a real dollar sales decline, infrastructure expansion continued, albeit rather slowly.

The findings for metropolitan counties with population decline help to resolve much of the ambiguity in the national trends. Such counties contain a very substantial proportion of the selected service industries, and their spending decline depressed the rate of growth for metropolitan areas in general. Population losses in metropolitan counties also reduced the rates of unit and employment change for metropolitan areas as a whole, though the impact was not as great. Thus, in metropolitan counties in general, the service infrastructure continued to grow at a relatively rapid rate. If the demand for services continues to decline in metropolitan counties with population losses, as seems likely, it is doubtful whether their service infrastructures will continue to expand. During the 1980s, metropolitan counties that continue to lose population are likely to experience service infrastructure contraction similar to that already evident in retailing.

Population and Retail Trends Since 1977

The Economic Census of 1977 is seven years old at this writing, and it will still be some time before 1982 data are available. Yet a great deal has happened both demographically and economically since 1977. In an effort to investigate recent trends, I have collected 1982 retail and population estimates for a stratified sample of 721 counties.[3] The retail estimates were prepared by Sales and Marketing Management Corporation and published in the 1983 *Survey of Buying Power* (Sales and Marketing Management, 1983). Such retail estimates for a sample of counties are certainly not as definitive as the census data for all U.S. counties used elsewhere in this study, so all figures presented here should be interpreted with some caution. Nonetheless, the data do indicate the likely patterns of recent demographic and retail change as well as the linkages between them.

Population Trends Since 1977

There is little question that the nonmetropolitan population turnaround continued between 1977 and 1982. An estimated 79 percent of all nonmetropolitan counties gained population between 1977 and 1982 (derived from Table 6.9)—a proportion roughly equal to the 80 percent that grew between 1970 and 1977. The pattern was much the same in metropolitan areas. An estimated 85 percent of metropolitan counties grew from 1977 to 1982, compared to 84 percent between 1970 and 1977.

Although the general patterns of population change observed in the 1970s continued into the 1980s, many individual counties changed the direction of their population shifts. The pattern of population change was most consistent among counties with histories of sustained population increase. Among both the metropolitan and nonmetropolitan groups with histories of population increase, over 92 percent of the counties continued to grow between 1977 and 1982 (Table 6.9). A large proportion (78.8 percent) of counties that began to grow between 1970 and 1977 after declining in previous decades also continued to grow between 1977 and 1982. In all, nearly 90 percent of the counties that grew between 1970 and 1977 continued to grow in the later period.

The pattern was less consistent among counties that lost population earlier in the 1970s. Just over 60 percent of both

TABLE 6.9
Population Change 1977 to 1982 for Counties Grouped by Comparing Historical Population Trends to Those Between 1970 and 1977

		Nonmetro Loss	Nonmetro Turnaround Gain	Nonmetro Turnaround Loss	Nonmetro Gain	Metro Decline	Metro Gain
Population Change 1977 – 1982	Population Decline	60.4%	21.2%	30.0%	5.2%	60.0%	7.2%
	Population Gain	39.6	78.8	70.0	94.8	40.0	92.8
		100.0% (419)	100.0% (869)	100.0% (71)	100.0% (1066)	100.0% (90)	100.0% (553)

Source: Census Bureau and Sales and Marketing Management Inc.

Note: Table based on weighted sample of 721 cases
Metro Status as of 1974

metropolitan and nonmetropolitan counties with histories of population loss continued to decline between 1977 and 1982. The least consistent counties were those that declined during the 1970s after growing in earlier decades. Only 30 percent of these counties continued to decline between 1977 and 1982. The inconsistency among such counties is not surprising, considering that they were running contrary to the national trend. Many apparently suffered short-term declines in the early 1970s before resuming growth later in the decade. In all, only 56 percent of the counties that declined between 1970 and 1977 continued to do so between 1977 and 1982.

In order to examine the linkages between population change and retail sales in the early 1980s, I have regrouped non-metropolitan counties by comparing the pattern of population change they experienced before 1970 with that between 1970 and 1982. I have also regrouped metropolitan counties according to the population change they experienced between 1970 and 1982.[4] This extension of the time frame for population change makes it possible to include more of the nonmetropolitan turnaround in the following analysis.

Between 1977 and 1982, population losses were greatest among nonmetropolitan counties with long histories of population decline. Counties in this group suffered an estimated aggregate loss of 5.8 percent of their 1977 population by 1982 (Table 6.10). By 1982 the average population of a county in this group was only 9205, its average retail sales only 33.3 million dollars. Significant population losses also occurred among the forty-nine counties that shifted to decline between 1970 and 1982 after growth before 1970. In metropolitan areas, ninety counties lost an estimated 2.1 million residents between 1977 and 1982, a net loss of 4.0 percent of their 1977 population. With few exceptions, these are the same metropolitan counties that lost population earlier in the decade.

In keeping with earlier findings, population gains in the late 1970s and early 1980s were greatest among nonmetro-politan counties with pre-1970 histories of population increase as well as among the 552 growing metropolitan counties. Nonmetropolitan gainers had an estimated population increase of over 4 million between 1977 and 1982, for an aggregate

TABLE 6.10
Mean Population and Retail Sales in 1982 and Aggregate Percentage Change in Population and Sales from 1977 to 1982 for Counties Grouped by Comparing Historical Population Trends to Those Between 1970 and 1982

	# of Counties	1982		1977 to 1982		
		Mean Population	Mean Sales	Population Change	Sales Change	Percent with Sales Gain
Nonmetro Loss	410	9,205	$ 33.3	-5.8%	-11.6%	8.0
Nonmetro Turnaround Gain	877	19,593	70.8	7.4%	- 5.8%	27.5
Nonmetro Turnaround Loss	49	23,899	118.2	-4.0%	-10.0%	17.6
Nonmetro Gain	1,089	36,271	148.8	11.4%	- 5.2%	29.1
Metro Declining	90	562,912	2,703.1	-4.0%	-10.3%	13.3
Metro Growing	553	235,608	1,196.2	11.6%	- 1.8%	37.1
All Sample Counties	3,068	79,055	374.3	7.3%	- 4.6%	26.6
U.S. Total	3,068	74,901	$ 353.7	8.3%	- 4.1%	na

Source: Population and sales estimates provided by Sales and Marketing Management, Inc.

Note: Sales in millions of 1982 dollars
  Percentage increase in sales is corrected for inflation
  Metro Status as of 1974
  U.S. Total reports summary data for the continental U.S.
  na = Data not available
  Table based on a weighted sample of 721 cases

gain of 11.4 percent; metropolitan gainers added 13.5 million
residents, for an aggregate gain of 11.6 percent. The counties
that shifted from population decline before 1970 to population
increase after 1970 continued to make significant gains between
1977 and 1982. Such counties had an aggregate population
gain of 7.4 percent, or about 1.2 million residents.

Among the sample counties population gains between 1977
and 1982 were greatest (10.0 percent) in nonmetropolitan
counties adjacent to metropolitan areas. Nonadjacent nonmetropolitan counties grew an estimated 7.4 percent, and
metropolitan counties gained 6.8 percent. Thus, the remarkable
reversal of long-term nonmetropolitan population trends appears to be continuing into the 1980s, although the gap
between the growth rates of metropolitan and nonmetropolitan
counties may be narrowing.[5]

Retail Trends Since 1977

During the early stages of the nonmetropolitan turnaround
(1970 to 1977), the retail and service sectors were strongly
influenced by the remarkable reversal of long-standing demographic trends. There was, in fact, a nonmetropolitan
business renaissance as well. The turnaround itself continued
in the late 1970s and early 1980s; did its influence on the
pattern of business change also continue?

Economically, the late 1970s and early 1980s have been
one of the most difficult periods since the Great Depression,
and inflation has been rampant. By 1982 the dollar was worth
only 60 percent of what it had been only five years earlier.
Such high inflation contributed to several severe recessions
that threw millions out of work and seriously depressed retail
spending. As a result, total retail sales in 1982 were 4 percent
lower than in 1977, after corrections are made for inflation.
To be sure, the inflation of the period pushed current dollar
retail spending up by nearly 50 percent, but the apparent
gains are illusionary, being purely a function of inflation.

Against this backdrop of economic recession and high
inflation, the widespread retail losses reported for the various
county groups between 1977 and 1982 become more com-

prehensible. Grouping the sample counties by metropolitan status and adjacency emphasizes the complexity of retail trends between 1977 and 1982. During this period metropolitan retail losses were smaller than those in nonmetropolitan areas, even though nonmetropolitan population gains continued to exceed those in metropolitan areas. Metropolitan areas had a real dollar retail sales decline of 2.3 percent between 1977 and 1982, nonmetropolitan nonadjacent counties lost an estimated 5.2 percent, and adjacent nonmetropolitan counties lost an estimated 6.5 percent. This pattern contrasts sharply with that between 1972 and 1977, when nonmetropolitan sales gains significantly exceeded those in metropolitan areas.

Other evidence also suggests that metropolitan areas may have weathered the economic storms of recent years somewhat better than nonmetropolitan areas. Nilsen (1984) has reported that nonmetropolitan unemployment rates exceed those in metropolitan areas. There has also been a substantial recent increase in the percentage of the nonmetropolitan population living below the poverty line. The gap between metropolitan and nonmetropolitan incomes has not narrowed since 1977, a departure from the historical convergence of metropolitan and nonmetropolitan incomes. Any analysis of the impact of recent population trends on the business structure must take into account this economic situation.

Retail data for the sample counties, grouped by comparing historical population trends to those between 1970 and 1982, leave little doubt that population change is continuing to exert a strong influence on retail sales, as it has both historically and during the earlier part of the turnaround. Growing metropolitan counties retained their traditional premier retail position between 1977 and 1982, though this means that they registered the smallest retail loss rather than the largest gain, as has historically been the case. Given the economic situation, the retail decrement of 1.8 percent suffered by such counties represents exceptional performance, as does the fact that 37 percent of the counties in this group actually registered a real dollar retail sales gain (Table 6.10). There is little question that the 11.6 percent population gain in such counties served to dampen the recession's impact on retailing.

The two groups of nonmetropolitan counties that gained population between 1970 and 1982 also had relatively small retail losses between 1977 and 1982. Nonmetropolitan continuing gainers suffered a retail loss of 5.2 percent, although 29 percent of the counties did enjoy retail growth. Turnaround gain counties suffered a slightly larger retail loss of 5.8 percent. As among metropolitan gainers, the large population increases in these county groups offset the difficult economic situation. However, other factors also influenced the rate of retail change. For instance, nonmetropolitan continuing gainers had a population gain of 11.4 percent, nearly equivalent to that of metropolitan gainers. Yet they suffered a substantially larger retail loss. In fact, nonmetropolitan turnaround gain counties lost only slightly more retail sales, despite a much smaller population gain (7.4 percent). The nonmetropolitan continuing gainers may have been hurt more by the economic downturn, though little evidence is as yet available to substantiate this speculation.

The interaction of population decline and a depressed economy is clearly reflected in the retail sales trends among counties that lost population. Nonmetropolitan counties with a history of population decline before and after 1970 suffered an aggregate loss of 11.6 percent between 1977 and 1982. Only 8 percent of these counties managed to achieve a retail sales gain—understandably, given the population decline. Nonmetropolitan turnaround loss counties also suffered a substantial retail sales loss due, at least in part, to population decline.

A large retail decline (10.3 percent) also accrued to metropolitan counties that lost population. Among such counties the sales decline resulting from the loss of population has been aggravated by the fact that many of those leaving are middle- and upper-income families shifting from older central cities or close-in suburbs to the outer fringes of the metropolitan area or beyond. Thus, the loss of retail purchasing power probably exceeds the loss of population. The estimated retail loss of 9.8 billion inflation-corrected dollars suffered by these ninety metropolitan counties between 1977 and 1982 is greater than the retail loss for all other U.S. counties combined. When one recalls that this retail loss comes on the heels of a similar retail loss among such metropolitan decliners between 1972 and 1977, it is not difficult to imagine the bleak future such areas face if the outflow of population does not subside.

Summary

The revival of population growth in the majority of the nation's nonmetropolitan counties stimulated a business renaissance as well. In both the retail and the service sectors sales gains between 1972 and 1977 were greater in nonmetropolitan areas than in the metropolitan centers that have traditionally dominated business. The fastest retail and service expansion still occurred in growing metropolitan counties, but business gains have also been large among nonmetropolitan counties with histories of population increase. The influence of the turnaround is also clearly reflected in the substantial retail and service gains among counties that began to gain population in the 1970s after losing residents before 1970. The smallest retail and service gains accrued to nonmetropolitan counties that lost population. Finally, declining metropolitan counties suffered an absolute loss of sales in both retail and service sectors between 1972 and 1977.

Infrastructure adjustments lag farther behind population change than do sales, so it will be some time before the full impact of the population turnaround on the nonmetropolitan infrastructure can be assessed. Preliminary evidence suggests that such adjustments are following the traditional pattern: infrastructure expansion was greatest among counties with sustained population increase and smallest among those with substantial population decline.

Sample data indicate that population increase remained widespread in nonmetropolitan areas during the late 1970s and early 1980s. There is also strong evidence that the pattern of population change in a county continued to influence local business trends between 1977 and 1982, despite the displacements caused by the worst economic conditions since the Great Depression.

Notes

1. The widespread decline in the number of retail establishments between 1972 and 1977 is a function of changes in the definition of retail establishments. The 1977 Retail Census does not include nonemployer direct sellers, whereas the 1972 Retail Census did. When the 1972 data are adjusted to exclude such firms and the percentage change in the number of retail establishments is recalculated, the figures show a gain of 4.2 percent between 1972 and 1977. Because nonemployer direct sellers are typically very small, excluding them makes less than .3 percent difference in total retail sales.

2. The slower rate of increase in service activity between 1972 and 1977 than between 1967 and 1972 is largely a statistical artifact. The Census Bureau expanded its definition of the Selected Service industry for the 1972 Economic Census, adding Legal Services, Dental Laboratories, and Engineering and Architectural firms. It is difficult to ascertain precisely what impact such revisions had on the various subgroups of counties. However, it is likely that the reported data modestly overestimate establishment and employment change and significantly overstate the increase in service expenditures between 1967 and 1972.

3. The sampling stratgey used was disproportionate stratified random sampling. The six county groups used as strata are those reported in Table 6.2. The number of counties selected and the proportion of all counties in the strata are:

Sample as Proportion of All Counties in the Group

	# of Sample Counties	% of Counties in the Group
Nonmetro Loss	91	21.7
Nonmetro Turnaround Gain	179	20.6
Nonmetro Turnaround Loss	40	56.2
Nonmetro Gain	210	19.7
Metro Declining	90	100.0
Metro Growing	111	20.1
Total Sample Counties	721	23.5

Counties are grouped by comparing historical population trends to those between 1970 and 1977.

All metropolitan declining counties are included because they are large and few in number. The inclusion or exclusion of one or two very large metropolitan counties might have seriously distorted the findings. Nonmetropolitan turnaround gain counties were disproportionately sampled because so few of them exist. Sample counties were then weighted to equal the original number of counties in that group.

4. The grouping procedures used here are the same as those used earlier in this chapter to examine retail and service trends between 1972 and 1977. The only difference is that the final period of population change here. is 1970 to 1982, rather than 1970 to 1977. This change resulted in shifts from one category to another for 17 percent of the counties. The remaining 83 percent remained in the same category they occupied when grouped according to population trends from 1970 to 1977.

5. Richter (1983) also suggests narrowing of the gap between metropolitan and nonmetropolitan population growth rates in the late 1970s. The data presented here support her finding that this reduced differential is primarily a function of a slower rate of population increase among nonadjacent nonmetropolitan counties, caused by lower levels of net migration gain. Despite this slowdown, Richter reports that nonmetropolitan growth rates still exceeded those in metropolitan areas between 1977 and 1980. Recent reports from the Bureau of the Census suggest that nonmetropolitan growth rates slowed even more during the 1980s. Forstall and Engels (1984) found that metropolitan growth exceeded nonmetropolitan growth by a small margin between 1980 and 1982. Such findings must be considered tentative until additional supporting evidence is presented, but they may indicate the onset of a period of equilibrium in the rate of population growth in metropolitan and nonmetropolitan areas that has been anticipated (Wardwell, 1977).

7
Summary and Implications

This study has focused on three key questions. First, what has been the historical pattern of demographic change in the nonmetropolitan United States? Second, how have historical population shifts influenced the local business infrastructure providing goods and services to nonmetropolitan residents? Finally, is the recent nonmetropolitan population turnaround affecting contemporary business development outside urban areas? This chapter summarizes the answers to these questions, and explores some of the implications of the findings.

Historical Demographic Trends in the Nonmetropolitan United States

Between 1920 and 1970 the United States was transformed from a predominantly rural to a largely urban nation, with the proportion of the population residing in nonmetropolitan areas falling from 50 percent to about 25 percent. While the rest of the nation experienced dramatic population growth, the nonmetropolitan population remained stable at approximately 54 million, despite substantial natural increase. Though few nonmetropolitan counties experienced either continuous growth or continuous decline over the whole fifty years, more than 35 percent lost population consistently from 1940 onward. By 1970, these counties were significantly smaller than they had been fifty years earlier. In contrast, 23 percent of all nonmetropolitan counties grew from 1940 onward, experiencing substantial population gains by 1970.

Migration was the primary mechanism of population redistribution, the dominant trend being a relentless exodus of people from rural areas. Although nearly universal, such migration losses were by no means uniform. Even many growing counties suffered net outmigration, though at rates substantially lower than in declining areas. Through most of the period from 1920 to 1970 the typical nonmetropolitan county gained population only when natural increase exceeded outmigration. In general, counties with heavy outmigration lost population; those with moderate or light outmigration grew. Not until the 1960s did a significant minority of growing counties experience inmigration, and then only as a supplement to natural increase.

The natural increase that pemitted many nonmetropolitan counties to grow despite significant outmigration was particularly high during the baby boom years of the fifties and early sixties. But the downturn in fertility during the late sixties deprived many nonmetropolitan counties of their traditional source of new population. As the surplus of births over deaths dwindled, a significant number of counties with prolonged population decline experienced natural decrease. This previously rare phenomenon was triggered by the cumulative effect of decades of age-specific outmigration coupled with the secular decline in fertility: the depleted ranks of young adults did not produce enough children to replace the losses suffered by a rapidly aging population.

A primary factor underlying rural-to-urban migration was the precipitous decline of the farm population, as mechanized equipment and improved technology replaced human labor in agriculture. The reduced demand for farm laborers, coupled with expanding employment opportunities in the industrial and business sectors of the urban economy, drained nearly 20 million people from the rural-farm population. Counties with protracted population decline had particularly heavy concentrations of agricultural workers and incurred staggering outmigration. The drain of rural-farm people started in the agricultural heartland of the Great Plains and Corn Belt and eventually spread to the Southern Coastal Plains and Mississippi Delta.

As counties dependent on agriculture contracted, those with a significant number of manufacturing jobs grew and prospered. Industrial firms were attracted to nonmetropolitan counties by inexpensive land, low taxes, and the large pool of low-wage nonunion workers, and later by the inducements of local government. The jobs they provided helped to stem the flow of migrants to urban areas. Although the proportion of the labor force engaged in manufacturing increased in each county group, the bulk of these jobs were concentrated in long-term growth counties. The shift of manufacturing jobs to nonmetropolitan areas started in the counties surrounding the urban industrial belts of the Midwest and Northeast, and later spread to the Southern Piedmont.

Population gains were also likely in counties with a significant concentration of urban residents. The large towns in such counties acted as service centers for the surrounding area and attracted new industrial and business facilities. Counties adjacent to metropolitan centers were also prone to grow, because of the spillover of urban population and the centrifugal forces stimulating economic growth at the metropolitan periphery. Growth was least likely in counties remote from metropolitan areas without any large urban places.

Counties rich in climate and recreational amenities also gained population as real income grew and leisure time increased. Such areas attracted migrants from the swelling ranks of affluent and mobile retirees, and were popular with the vacationing public; the resulting increased demand for goods and services reduced the outflow of residents by providing jobs locally. Florida and the Southwest have long attracted migrants to their mild climates and recreational amenities, and recent growth in portions of the Upland South and Upper Midwest has also been stimulated by these factors. The trends reflected in these data were forerunners of the nonmetropolitan population turnaround of the 1970s.

The Impact of Population Change
on Nonmetropolitan Business

The local business infrastructure adjusted to population change through changes in scale, number of employees, and number of establishments, although efforts to trace this process are complicated by other causal factors that increased the demand for retail goods and services in all counties. Retail data confirm that population change stimulates organizational modification and that such modification becomes more pronounced as the magnitude and duration of consistent population change increase. Population change exerted a strong direct influence on retail sales; its impact on establishment change was even stronger, and included an indirect effect through sales change as well as a direct effect. Retail employment was also heavily influenced by population shifts, though the effect was totally indirect, mediated by sales and establishment change.

Retail sales increased in each county group between 1929 and 1972 regardless of population gain or loss. These retail gains resulted from the substantial growth of per capital retail expenditures stimulated by the doubling of real family income. Though this sales expansion complicates the analytical problem, it does not nullify the effect of population change on retailing. Sales gains were greatest in protracted-growth counties, where the general increase in per capita spending was multiplied by a rapidly expanding population. In declining counties, modest sales gains were possible only because higher per capita retail expenditures offset the loss of consumers.

Organizational modifications in response to population change included adjustments in both the number and the operational scale of retail units. Prolonged growth stimulated establishment gains, whereas extended loss resulted in unit reductions. Resistance to establishment change is reflected in unit adjustments that were less than proportionate to incremental change in either retail sales or population itself. The data analyzed in this study do not allow a complete exploration of the reasons underlying this resistance, but both the significant capital commitments involved in opening or closing units and the personal adjustments required of proprietors are known to be important.

The spiraling demand for retail goods, coupled with organizational resistance to establishment change, resulted in an expanded scale of operations among units whether county populations grew or declined. The expansion was greatest in growing counties, where the few additional retail units were not sufficient to accommodate the surge in demand without scale adjustment, but even in declining counties fewer units had to handle more sales.

The reliance on scale adjustments to accommodate demand shifts may well derive from the ease and speed with which the former can be accomplished. The principal means of reconciling operational scale to demand is through incremental adjustments in the size of the labor force. Such adjustments could be accomplished easily in nonmetropolitan areas because of the surplus of low-wage workers suitable for unskilled retail positions. This flexibility underlay the widespread resistance to proportionate shifts in the number of retail units in response to population change. Scale expansion thus led, in each county group, to employment gains—greatest in counties with protracted population gain and least in long-term loss counties.

In contrast to the mature retail industry, the selected services were still in their infancy in the 1930s and expanded rapidly during the study period as new services became available. The increased demand for such services is reflected in per capita spending gains much more than proportionate to the rise in incomes. As a result, service receipts rose spectacularly, stimulating organizational expanison in each county group. Populaton change dampened the expansion in protracted-decline counties and accelerated it in prolonged-growth counties.

The organizational expansion required to accommodate the surging demand for services increased both the scale and the number of units everywhere, and there was little resistance to adjustments in the number of establishments. The magnitude of employment and estblishment gains depended on the direction, duration, and rate of population change. Prolonged population decline did not completely offset per capita spending gains, but did reduce service sector expansion. By the same token, gains were greatest in prolonged-growth counties, where the general per capital spending increase was multiplied by a growing population.

The absence of resistance to establishment change resulted in a balanced organizational response, encompassing significant increases in both employees and establishments. The scale of operations of service units also increased substantially, but in most counties the demand increments simply overwhelmed the system's capacity to respond through scale shifts. The result was a proliferation of small, owner-operated units.

The Population Turnaround and Its Impact on Business

The remarkable reversal of nonmetropolitan population trends since 1970 represents a fundamental break from the dominant demographic pattern of the last hundred years. Traditionally, most nonmetropolitan counties lost population to the urban centers that dominate the nation both demographically and economically. However, since 1970 nearly 80 percent of the nonmetropolitan counties have been gaining population. Such growth is most common among nonmetropolitan counties with long histories of population increase, but it is even occurring in a majority of the counties that consistently lost population for forty or more years before 1970. In recent years nonmetropolitan population gains actually exceeded those in metropolitan areas by a significant margin, an occurrence virtually unheard of in U.S. demographic history. This reversal is occurring among both adjacent and nonadjacent nonmetropolitan counties and in every geographic region of the nation. Sample data suggest that it is persisting into the early 1980s, confirming that it is more than a short-term perturbation in a long-term trend.

Much of the impetus for this growth has come from migration—in particular, from net inmigration to nearly 65 percent of the nonmetropolitan counties since 1970. Net inmigration was unusual in nonmetropolitan areas before 1970, even among counties with increasing population. Historically, nonmetropolitan counties have grown when gains from natural increase exceeded losses from outmigration. But since 1970 nonmetropolitan population gains from migration have roughly matched those from natural increase, both because nonmetropolitan areas are attracting migrants, and because they are retaining more of their existing residents. These migration gains are extremely widespread, occurring among both adjacent and nonadjacent nonmetropolitan counties.

This influx of migrants comes at a time when nonmetropolitan gains from natural increase are at a low ebb, not only because of shifts in fertility behavior but also because age-selective outmigration has distorted the age structure in many nonmetropolitan areas. This distortion is reflected in a high incidence of natural decrease, particularly among counties with long histories of population decline. In general, the reduced contribution of natural increase, coupled with significant inmigration in many counties, represents a clear break with the past pattern of nonmetropolitan growth through an excess of natural increase over outmigration.

Demographers are still sorting out the factors underlying this remarkable reversal of long-standing population trends. Part of the nonmetropolitan gain represents a spillover of metropolitan growth into adjacent nonmetropolitan counties, a continuation of the metropolitan peripheral expansion known to have been occurring for some time. However, the turnaround is more than an artifact of urban spillover. In many cases growth has been more rapid among counties distant from metropolitan areas and without any large urban place. And with few exceptions it has been such remote places that have reaped the greatest benefits from inmigration.

Many of these nonmetropolitan inmigrants are coming from urban areas. Some desire a different style of life, others are retiring from urban jobs, and still others seek the economic opportunities available in nonmetropolitan areas. Whatever their reasons for coming, these newcomers have made a significant contribution to the revival of growth in some nonmetropolitan areas with long histories of decline.

The nonmetropolitan population turnaround stimulated a rural business renaissance as well. Nonmetropolitan sales gains exceeded those in metropolitan areas between 1972 and 1977 in both the retail and the service sectors. In nonmetropolitan areas the greatest sales gains were among counties with long histories of population increase and among turnaround counties that began to gain population in the 1970s after earlier losses. Metropolitan counties that gained population had the largest sales gains, whereas metropolitan counties that lost population suffered the greatest sales losses. Thus, changes in the size of the proximate population continued to affect the local demand for goods and services in the 1970s, just as they have historically.

The business infrastructure appears to be responding to the demand shifts resulting from the post-1970 revival of population increase in nonmetropolitan areas. The turnaround is so recent that its influence on business is only beginning to become evident; however, the character of the resulting infrastructure adjustments appears to be consistent with historical trends. Expanison was greatest among counties with sustained population increase and smallest among those with substantial population decline, and the scale of operations among units continued to grow. There is evidence of a lag between the onset of population change and infrastructure adjustments to it. This lag is also consistent with the historical patterns reported earlier, and reinforces the point that it will be some time before the full impact of the turnaround of the business infrastructure can be assessed.

The impact of the population turnaround on nonmetropolitan business trends between 1977 and 1982 is more difficult to gauge. The turnaround itself appears to be continuing, and it continued to influence retail sales despite the reduced spending levels in recent years resulting from the depressed economy and high inflation. Population gains dampened retail losses, and population decline accelerated them. However, in contrast to the situation during the earlier part of the turnaround, retail losses were smaller in metropolitan counties despite the larger population gains in nonmetropolitan areas. This difference was due primarily to the minimal retail losses suffered by metropolitan counties that gained population, which buoyed up the overall metropolitan performance. However, it serves to emphasize the point that a variety of factors in addition to population change continue to influence retailing.

Future Trends

It is difficult to predict whether nonmetropolitan counties will continue to be among the fastest growing retail and service markets during the 1980s. The gap between the rates of population increase in metropolitan and nonmetropolitan areas narrowed in the late 1970s, and may close during the 1980s. There is little chance that demographic trends will revert to the pre-1970 pattern, however, because the economic and industrial structure of contemporary nonmetropolitan counties is quite different from that of earlier times. Population growth is likely to continue in most nonmetropolitan counties during the 1980s and may be rapid in many. Substantial population gains are also likely in small metropolitan areas and in selected major metropolitan markets. Other large metropolitan markets, particularly in the Midwest and Northeast, will not do as well because although gentrification is bringing some of the affluent customers retailers treasure back to selected big-city neighborhoods, it has done little to stem the exodus of middle-class families to the suburbs and beyond. Responding to such population trends, a growing number of retail and service firms are likely to continue to expand their activities in nonmetropolitan and middle markets during the 1980s.

The economy is the biggest unknown affecting predictions about the future expansion of the nonmetropolitan business structure. Population change is an important factor fueling retail and service expansion, but it is by no means the only significant factor. Nonmetropolitan areas have been hit hard by the nation's recent economic difficulties. Even though population gains in nonmetropolitan areas continued to exceed metropolitan gains between 1977 and 1982, the metropolitan business sector weathered the economic downturn better. Continued nonmetropolitan business growth depends on a healthy national economy.

The attitudes of nonmetropolitan residents also affect the future growth of retail trade. Most people welcome the selection and competition fostered by retail expansion, but the feeling is not universal. Established small-town retailers often have difficulty competing with the modern marketing practices of the expanding chains.

In addition, many new units are built in shopping malls beyond the edge of town. Sometimes the new malls drain sales tax revenue from hard-pressed rural towns and hasten the demise of older, downtown retail districts. When an old shopping area is simply exchanged for a newer one, no dramatic growth in retail sales occurs.

Although the new retail trends are important, the bulk of population is, and will remain, metropolitan. Sales outside metropolitan areas still constitute only 25 percent of the U.S. total. But as traditional markets reach saturation and the pressure on retail firms to expand continues, it is likely that attention will turn increasingly to new markets. And many of those new markets lie beyond the metropolitan borders.

Conclusion

The principal theoretical contribution of this study comes from its focus on delineating the impact of population change on components of the organizational structure in nonmetropolitan counties. Traditionally, population has not been considered an independent variable in ecological research. Rather, it has been seen to occur in response to shifts in the organizational structure of a system, or as a result of drastic environmental change. Although this study does not address the question of whether population can initiate change, it assumes that the causal linkages among components of the ecological complex are not unidirectional. A change in one segment of the structure may, after reverberating through the system, eventually require additional change in the originating segment. Thus, the fact that population change was caused by prior organizational change does not negate its role as an independent variable. By accepting population change as a causal agent, we can investigate topics neglected by researchers intent on determining what factors caused population change. Specifically, by delineating how population change affected the local business structure, which is heavily dependent on the proximate population for patronage, the study contributes valuable information about the organizational adjustment process. The results will be useful to researchers investigating the social, economic, and policy implications of the revival of growth in nonmetropolitan areas.

Nonmetropolitan research has long been limited by the paucity of data before 1950. By extending the analysis back several decades, this study contributes valuable information about nonmetropolitan demographic and business changes early in this century. Using an extended time frame also allows us to examine the long-term effects of population change on the retail and service sectors.

This research documents the strong influence population change exerts on the business infrastructure developed to deliver goods and services to nonmetropolitan residents. It demonstrates that population change may appropriately be used as an independent variable under some conditions in ecological research. And it confirms the ecological expectation that change in one component of the ecological complex cannot long prevail without concomitant changes in other ecological components. The evidence also suggests that organizational expansion and contraction are not symmetrical. If a growing system later contracts, it does so through a different process. This finding is in keeping with the ecological tenet that system change is irreversible.

The way in which the business infrastructure responds to population change is neither simple nor immediate. The process of adjustment is complex, because a variety of other causal agents also exert an independent effect on the demand for goods and services and the infrastructure that provides them.

Organizational adjustments are not immediate, because the system has adequate flexibility to tolerate short-term demand fluctuations without significant structural adjustment. But sustained population change does cause local business infrastructure modification. The influence of population change on the local business infrastructure is evident through nearly sixty years of recent U.S. history, including periods of economic expansion and contraction as well as a remarkable reversal of long-standing demographic trends. It must be taken seriously by anyone who seeks to understand the business structure providing goods and services to nonmetropolitan Americans.

Appendix

Population Change, Net Migration, and Natural Increase 1970 to 1975 for Counties
with Histories of Population Change, by Metropolitan Adjacency, and Size of Largest Place

	Population Change		Net Migration		Natural Increase		
	Percent Change	Percent Growing	Percent Change	Percent Gaining	Percent Change	Percent Gaining	
All Nonmetropolitan							
Adj-Large Urb	9.6	89	4.8	61	4.9	96	(253)
Adj-Small Urb	10.1	87	6.3	73	3.9	87	(702)
Nonadj-Large Urb	8.4	85	2.9	64	5.5	98	(264)
Nonadj-Small Urb	8.5	73	4.9	62	3.6	81	(1,206)
All	9.2	80	4.7	65	4.4	86	(2,425)
Protracted Loss							
Adj-Large Urb	2.2	50	1.9	50	0.3	63	(8)
Adj-Small Urb	2.7	69	1.1	58	1.6	67	(137)
Nonadj-Large Urb	-1.5	44	-4.8	11	3.3	67	(9)
Nonadj-Small Urb	1.2	48	0.3	46	0.9	58	(324)
All Protracted Loss	1.6	54	0.4	49	1.2	61	(478)
Short Term Loss							
Adj-Large Urb	4.2	84	0.0	38	4.2	100	(50)
Adj-Small Urb	6.0	78	2.2	61	3.8	93	(193)
Nonadj-Large Urb	5.2	77	0.4	54	4.8	99	(79)
Nonadj-Small Urb	6.2	74	2.4	58	3.8	89	(488)
All Short Term Loss	5.6	76	1.5	57	4.1	91	(810)
Short Term Gain							
Adj-Large Urb	10.2	88	6.2	70	4.0	91	(43)
Adj-Small Urb	12.4	98	8.7	86	3.8	90	(244)
Nonadj-Large Urb	6.7	87	1.9	68	4.8	99	(71)
Nonadj-Small Urb	13.4	93	9.3	79	4.1	92	(305)
All Short Term Gain	11.2	94	7.1	80	4.1	92	(663)
Long Term Gain							
Adj-Large Urb	11.0	92	5.6	66	5.4	99	(152)
Adj-Small Urb	14.4	97	9.4	81	5.0	95	(128)
Nonadj-Large Urb	11.9	93	5.4	72	6.5	99	(105)
Nonadj-Small Urb	15.8	96	9.8	84	5.9	93	(89)
All Long Term Gain	12.3	94	6.6	75	5.7	97	(474)

Note: Percent Change represents the total percentage change in the specific group of counties
for given population component.
Percent Gaining represents the percentage of the counties gaining residents through the
given population component.
Protracted Loss group includes counties with losses beginning before 1940.
Short Term Loss group includes counties with losses beginning in 1940 or later.
Short Term Gain group includes counties with consistent growth beginning in 1940 or after.
Long Term Gain group includes counties with consistent gain beginning before 1940.
Large Urban groups include counties with an urban place of at least 10,000 in 1970.

Bibliography

Adams, Bert N. 1969. "The Small Trade Center: Processes and Perceptions of Growth or Decline." In *The Community*, ed. Robert M. French. Itasca, IL: Peacock.

Alonso, William, and Edgar Rust. 1975. *Life in the Economically Declining Parts of Montana, North Dakota and Wyoming*. Berkeley, CA: Berkeley Planning Associates.

Anderson, A. H. 1950. "Space as a Social Cost." *Journal of Farm Economics* 32:411–430.

———. 1961. *The 'Expanding' Rural Community*. Lincoln: Nebraska Agricultural Experiment Station Bulletin 464.

Anderson, T. R., and J. Collier. 1956. "Metropolitan Dominance and the Rural Hinterland." *Rural Sociology* 21:152–157.

Beale, Calvin L. 1964. "Rural Depopulation in the United States: Some Demographic Consequences of Agricultural Adjustments." *Demography* 1:264–272.

———. 1969. "Natural Decrease of Population: The Current and Prospective Status of an Emergent American Phenomenon." *Demography* 6:91–99.

———. 1974. "Quantitative Dimensions of Decline and Stability Among Rural Communities." In *Communities Left Behind: Alternatives for Development*, ed. Larry R. Whiting. Ames: Iowa State University Press.

———. 1975. *The Revival of Population Growth in Nonmetropolitan America*. Washington, D.C.: Economic Research Service, U.S. Department of Agriculture, ERS-605.

———. 1978. "People on the Land." In *Rural U.S.A.: Persistence and Change*, ed. Thomas R. Ford. Ames: Iowa State University Press.

Beale, Calvin L., and Glenn V. Fuguitt. 1975. *Recent Nonmetropolitan Population Trends in the United States*. Washington, D.C.: Economic Research Service, U.S. Department of Agriculture.

165

————. 1976. *The New Pattern of Nonmetropolitan Population Change.* Madison, WI: Center for Demography and Ecology, No. 75-22.

Bender, Lloyd D. 1980. "The Effect of Trends in Economic Structure on Population Change in Rural Areas." In *New Directions in Urban-Rural Migration*, ed. David L. Brown and John M. Wardwell. New York: Academic Press.

Berry, Brian L. 1973. *Growth Centers in the American Urban System.* Cambridge, MA: Ballinger.

Bertrand, Alvin L. 1978. "Rural Social Organizational Implications of Technology and Industry." In *Rural U.S.A.: Persistence and Change*, ed. Thomas R. Ford. Ames: Iowa State University Press.

Biggar, Jeanne C. 1979. *The Sunning of America: Migration to the Sunbelt.* New York: Population Reference Bureau, Population Bulletin 34-1.

Blackwood, Larry G., and Edwin H. Carpenter. 1978. "The Importance of Anti-Urbanism in Determining Residential Preferences and Migration Patterns." *Rural Sociology* 43(1):31–47.

Blau, Peter. 1970. "A Formal Theory of Differentiation in Organizations." *American Sociological Review* 35:201–218.

Bluestone, Herman. 1970. *Focus for Area Development Analysis: Urban Orientation of Counties.* Washington, D.C.: Economic Research Service, U.S. Department of Agriculture, AER-183.

Bogue, Donald J. 1959. *The Population of the United States.* Glencoe, IL: Free Press.

Bollinger, W. Lamar. 1972. "The Economic and Social Impact of the Depopulation Process Upon Four Selected Counties in Idaho." In *Commission on Population Growth and the American Future*, ed. Sara Mills Mazie. Washington: GPO.

Bowles, Gladys K. 1978. "Contributions of Recent Metro/Nonmetro Migrants to the Nonmetro Population and Labor Force." *Agricultural Economics Research* 30:15–22.

Brown, David L. 1974. "The Redistribution of Physicians and Dentists in Incorporated Places of the Upper Midwest, 1950–1970." *Rural Sociology* 39:205–223.

————. 1975. *Socioeconomic Characteristics of Growing and Declining Nonmetropolitan Counties, 1970.* Washington, D.C.: Economic Research Service, U.S. Department of Agriculture, AER-306.

————. 1981. "Some Spatial Aspects of Work Force Migration in the United States, 1965–1975." Presented at the Annual Meetings of the Population Association of America, Atlanta, GA.

Brown, David L., and Calvin L. Beale. 1981. "Diversity of Post-1970 Population Trends." In *Nonmetropolitan America in Tran-*

sition, ed. Amos H. Hawley and Sarah Mills Mazie. Chapel Hill: University of North Carolina Press.

Brown, David L., and John M. Wardwell, eds. 1980. *New Directions in Urban-Rural Migration*. New York: Academic Press.

Brunner, Edmund deS. 1951. "Village Growth 1940–1950." *Rural Sociology* 16:111–118.

Brunner, Edmund deS., G. S. Hughes, and M. Patten. 1927. *American Agricultural Villages*. New York: George H. Doran Co.

Brunner, Edmund deS., and John H. Kolb. 1933. *Rural Social Trends*. New York: McGraw-Hill.

Brunner, Edmund deS., and Irving Lorge. 1937. *Rural Trends in the Depression Years*. New York: Columbia University Press.

Campbell, Rex R. 1975. "Beyond the Suburbs: The Changing Rural Scene." In *Metropolitan America*, ed. Amos H. Hawley and Vincent Rock. Washington, D.C.: National Academy of Sciences.

Carlsson, Gosta. 1968. "Change, Growth and Irreversibility." *American Journal of Sociology* 73:706–714.

Carpenter, Harold R. 1974. "Enhancing Social Opportunity." In *Communities Left Behind: Alternatives for Development*, ed. Larry R. Whiting. Ames: Iowa State University Press.

Chang, H. C. 1974. "Natural Population Decrease in Iowa Counties." *Demography* 11:657–672.

Cottrell, W. F. 1951. "Death by Dieselization: A Case Study in the Reaction to Technological Change." *American Sociological Review* 16:358–365.

Daily, George H., Jr., and Rex R. Campbell. 1980. "The Ozark-Ouachita Uplands: Growth and Consequences." In *New Directions in Urban-Rural Migration*, ed. David L. Brown and John M. Wardwell. New York: Academic Press.

Doeksen, Gerald A., John Kuehn, and Joseph Schmidt. 1974. "Consequences of Decline and Community Economic Adjustment to It." In *Communities Left Behind: Alternatives for Development*, ed. Larry R. Whiting. Ames: Iowa State University Press.

Doerflinger, Jon, and Jeffrey Robinson. 1962. *The Impact of Population Change on Rural Community Life: The Government, Health and Welfare Systems*. Ames: Iowa State University Press.

Dorn, H. E. 1936. "The Natural Decrease of Population in Certain American Communities." *Journal of the American Statistical Association*. 34:106–109.

Eldridge, H. T., and D. S. Thomas. 1964. "Demographic Analyses and Interrelations." In *Population Redistribution and Economic*

Growth, United States, 1870–1950, ed. S. Kuznets and D. S. Thomas. Philadelphia: The American Philosophical Society.

Ellenbogen, Bert L. 1974. "Service Structure of the Small Community: Problems and Options for Change." In *Communities Left Behind: Alternatives for Development,* ed. Larry R. Whiting. Ames: Iowa State University Press.

Forstall, R. L., and R. A. Engels. 1984. "Growth In Nonmetropolitan Areas Slows." Washington, D.C.: Bureau of the Census. Unpublished manuscript.

Fox, Karl A., and T. Krishna Kumar. 1965. "The Functional Economic Area: Delineation and Implications for Economic Analysis and Policy." *Papers of the Regional Science Association* 15:57–85.

Freeman, John, and Michael Hanna. 1975. "Growth and Decline Processes in Organizations." *American Sociological Review* 40:215–228.

Frisbie, W. Parker, and Dudley L. Poston, Jr. 1975. "Components of Sustenance Organization and Nonmetropolitan Population Change: A Human Ecological Investigation." *American Sociological Review* 40:773–784.

———. 1978. *Sustenance Organization and Population Redistribution in Nonmetropolitan America.* Iowa City: University of Iowa Press.

Fuguitt, Glenn V. 1965a. "The Growth and Decline of Small Towns as a Probability Process." *American Sociological Review* 30:403–411.

———. 1965b. "The Small Town in Rural America." *Journal of Cooperative Extension* 25:19–26.

———. 1965c. "County Seat Status as a Factor in Small Town Growth and Decline." *Social Forces* 44:245–251.

———. 1971. "The Places Left Behind: Population Trends and Policy for Rural America." *Rural Sociology* 36:449–470.

Fuguitt, Glenn V., and Nora Ann Deeley. 1966. "Retail Service Patterns and Small Town Population Change: A Replication of Hassinger's Study." *Rural Sociology* 31:53–63.

Fuguitt, Glenn V., and James J. Zuiches. 1972. *Nonmetropolitan Cities of Sustained Growth or Chronic Decline.* Madison: Center for Demography and Ecology, 72–77.

———. 1975. "Residential Preferences and Population Distribution." *Demography* 12:491–504.

Galpin, Charles J. 1915. *The Social Anatomy of an Agricultural Community.* Madison: Wisconsin Agricultural Experiment Station Bulletin 34.

Gardner, J., and W. Cohen. 1971. "County Level Demographic Characteristics of the Population of the United States, 1930 to 1950." Unpublished manuscript. Ann Arbor, MI: Inter-University Consortium for Political and Social Research.

Gibbs, Jack P., and Walter T. Martin. 1959. "Toward a Theoretical System of Human Ecology." *Pacific Sociological Review* 2:29–36.

Gray, Irwin. 1969. "Employment Effect of a New Industry in a Rural Area." *Monthly Labor Review* 92(6):26–30.

Greenwood, Michael J. 1975. "Simultaneity Bias in Migration Models: An Empirical Examination." *Demography* 12:519–536.

Guest, Avery M., and Christopher Cluett. 1974. "Metropolitan Retail Nucleation." *Demography* 11:493–507.

Haas, Eugene, Richard H. Hall, and Norman Johnson. 1963. "The Size of the Supportive Component in Organizations: A Multi-organizational Analysis." *Social Forces* 42:9–17.

Hamilton, C. H., and F. M. Henderson. 1944. "Use of the Survival Rate Method in Measuring Net Migration." *Journal of the American Statistical Association* 39:197–206.

Hansen, Niles M. 1973. *The Future of Nonmetropolitan America: Studies in the Reversal of Rural and Small Town Population Decline.* Lexington, MA: Lexington Books.

Hassinger, Edward. 1957a. "The Relationship of Retail Service Patterns to Trade Center Population Change." *Rural Sociology* 22:235–240.

_____. 1957b. "The Relationship of Trade-Center Population Change to Distance from Larger Centers in an Agricultural Area." *Rural Sociology* 22:131–136.

Hassinger, Edward, and Robert L. McNamara. 1956. "The Pattern of Medical Services for Incorporated Places of 500-or-more Population in Missouri, 1950." *Rural Sociology* 21:175–177.

Hathaway, Dale E. 1960. "Migration from Agriculture: The Historical Record and its Meaning." *American Economic Review* 150:379–391.

Hawley, Amos H. 1950. *Human Ecology.* New York: Ronald Press.

_____. 1971. *Urban Society.* New York: Ronald Press.

_____. 1973. "Ecology." Chapel Hill: University of North Carolina. Unpublished manuscript.

_____. 1976. "Spatial Aspects of Population: An Overview." Chapel Hill: University of North Carolina. Unpublished manuscript.

Hines, Fred K., David L. Brown, and John M. Zimmer. 1975. *Social and Economic Characteristics of the Population in Metro and*

Nonmetro Counties, 1970. Washington, D.C.: Economic Research Service, U.S. Department of Agriculture, AER-272.

Hirsch, Werner Z. 1961. "Measuring Local Services." In *Exploring the Metropolitan Community,* ed. John C. Bollents. Berkeley and Los Angeles: University of California Press.

Hodge, Gerald. 1965. "The Prediction of Trade Center Viability in the Great Plains." *Papers of the Regional Science Association* 15:87–115.

Hoffer, Charles R. 1935. *Changes in the Retail and Service Facilities of Rural Trade Centers in Michigan, 1900–1930.* East Lansing: Michigan State College Agricultural Extension Service, SB-261.

Humphrey, Craig R., and Ralph R. Sell. 1975. "The Impact of Controlled Access Highways on Population Growth in Pennsylvania Nonmetropolitan Communities, 1940–1970." *Rural Sociology* 40:332–343.

Johansen, Harley E., and Glenn V. Fuguitt. 1973. "Changing Retail Activity in Wisconsin Villages: 1939–1954–1970." *Rural Sociology* 38:207–218.

———. 1979. "Population Growth and Rural Decline: Conflicting Effects of Urban Accessibility in American Villages." *Rural Sociology* 44:24–38.

———. 1984. *The Changing Rural Village in America.* Cambridge, MA: Ballinger.

Johnson, Kenneth M. 1980. "Impact of Population Change on Retail and Selected Services in Nonmetropolitan American Counties, 1920–1972." Ph.D. dissertation, University of North Carolina at Chapel Hill.

———. 1981. "The Rural Population Renaissance in Historical Perspective: Nonmetropolitan Population and Migration Trends, 1930 to 1980." Paper presented at the Annual Meeting of the Population Association of America, Washington, D.C.

———. 1982a. "Organizational Adjustment to Population Change in Nonmetropolitan America: A Longitudinal Analysis of Retail Trade." *Social Forces* 60:1123–1139.

———. 1982b. "Rural Retailing Reborn." *American Demographics,* September.

Johnson, Kenneth M., and Ross L. Purdy. 1980. "Recent Nonmetropolitan Population Change in Fifty Year Perspective." *Demography* 17:57–70.

Klietsch, Ronald G. 1962. *The Impact of Population Change on Rural Community Life—The School System.* Ames: Iowa State University Press.

Lee, Everett S., Ann R. Miller, Carol P. Brainerd, and Richard A. Easterlin. 1957. *Population Redistribution and Economic Growth, United States, 1870–1950*. Philadelphia: The American Philosophical Society.

Lord, J. D. 1982. "Intercounty Retail Leakage Patterns in North Carolina." *Southeastern Geographer* 22:52–67.

Lowenthal, David, and Lambros Comitas. 1962. "Emigration and Depopulation: Some Neglected Aspects of Population Geography." *The Geographical Review* 12:195–210.

Maddox, James G. 1960. "Private and Social Costs of the Movement of People out of Agriculture." *American Economic Review* 150:392–401.

Markides, Krysikos S., and George S. Tracy. 1977. "Natural Population Decrease and the Theory of Demographic Response." Paper presented at the Annual Meetings of the Population Association of America, St. Louis.

Meyer, Marshall. 1972. "Size and Structure of Organizations: A Causal Analysis." *American Sociological Review* 37:434–440.

Morrison, Peter A., with Judith P. Wheeler. 1976. *Rural Renaissance in America? The Revival of Population Growth in Remote Areas*. New York: Population Reference Bureau, Population Bulletin 31–3.

Nelson, Lowry, and Ernst T. Jacobson. 1941. "Recent Changes in Farm Trade Centers in Minnesota." *Rural Sociology* 6:99–106.

Nilsen, Sigurd R. 1984. "Recessionary Impacts on the Unemployment of Men and Women." *Monthly Labor Review*, May, pp. 21–25.

North Central Regional Center for Rural Development. 1973. *Rural Development: Research Priorities*. Ames: Iowa State University Press.

_____. 1974. *Rural Industrialization: Problems and Potentials*. Ames: Iowa State University Press.

Northam, Ray M. 1963. "Declining Urban Centers in the United States: 1940–1960." *Annals of the Association of American Geographers* 53:50–59.

_____. 1969. "Population Size, Relative Location and Declining Urban Centers: Coterminous United States, 1940–1960." *Land Economics* 45:313–322.

Ploch, Louis A. 1980. "Effects of Turnaround Migration on Community Structure in Maine." In *New Directions in Urban-Rural Migration*, ed. David L. Brown and John M. Wardwell. New York: Academic Press.

Purdy, Ross L. 1976. "Demographic Aspects of Depopulation 1890–
1970." Chapel Hill: University of North Carolina. Unpublished
manuscript.

Raup, Phillip. 1961. "Economic Aspects of Population Decline in
Rural Communities." In *Labor Mobility and Population in Agri-
culture.* Ames: Iowa State University Center for Agriculture and
Economic Adjustment.

Richardson, Joseph L., and Olaf F. Larson. 1976. "Small Community
Trends." *Rural Sociology* 41:45–59.

Richter, Kerry. 1983. *Nonmetropolitan Growth in the Late 1970's: The
End of the Turnaround?* Madison, WI: Center for Demography
and Ecology, 83-10.

Rockwell, Richard C. 1975. "Assessment of Multicollinearity: The
Haitovsky Test of the Determinate." *Sociological Methods and
Research* 3:308–320.

Rogers, D. L., B. F. Pendleton, W. J. Goudy, and R. O. Richards.
1978. "Industrialization, Income Benefits, and Rural Community."
Rural Sociology 43(2):250–264.

Rundbald, Bengt G. 1957. "Problems of a Depopulated Rural
Community." In *Migration in Sweden: A Symposium*, ed. David
Hannenbert. Lund, Sweden: Royal University of Lund, No. 12.

Rust, Edgar. 1975. *No Growth: Impacts on Metropolitan Areas.*
Lexington, MA: D. C. Heath.

Sales and Marketing Management. 1983. *Survey of Buying Power.*
New York: Bill.

Scott, John T., Jr., and James D. Johnson. 1976. *The Effect of Town
Size and Location on Retail Sales.* Ames, IA: North Central Regional
Center for Rural Development.

Shane, Matthew. 1972. *The Flow of Funds through the Commercial
Banking System, Minnesota–North Dakota.* Minneapolis: Minnesota
Agricultural Experimental Station Bulletin 506.

Simon, William, and John H. Gagon. 1967. "The Decline and Fall
of the Small Town." In *The Community*, ed. Robert M. French.
Itasca, IL: Peacock.

Smith, T. Lynn. 1942. "The Role of the Village in American Rural
Society." *Rural Sociology* 7:16–18.

———. 1969. "A Study of Social Stratification in the Agricultural
Sections of the U.S." *Rural Sociology* 34:498–509.

Stuby, Richard G. 1976. "The Relationship between Structural
Differentiation and Selected Population Variables." Paper pre-
sented at the Annual Meeting of the Rural Sociological Society,
New York.

Sundquist, James L. 1975. *Dispersing Population: What Americans Can Learn from Europe.* Washington, D.C.: Brookings Institution.

Tarver, J. D. 1972. "Patterns of Population Change among Southern Nonmetropolitan Towns, 1950–1970." *Rural Sociology* 37:553–572.

Tarver, James D., and Calvin L. Beale. 1968. "Population Trends of Southern Nonmetropolitan Towns." *Rural Sociology* 33:19–29.

Taves, Marvin J. 1961. "Consequences of Population Loss in Rural Communities." In *Labor Mobility and Population in Agriculture.* Ames: Iowa State University Center for Agriculture and Economic Adjustment.

Terrien, Frederick W., and Donald L. Mills. 1955. "The Effect of Changing Size upon the Internal Structure of Organizations." *American Sociological Review* 20:11–23.

Tucker, C. Jack. 1976. "Changing Patterns of Migration Between Metropolitan and Nonmetropolitan Areas in the United States: Recent Evidence." *Demography* 13:435–443.

Uhlenberg, Peter. 1973. "Noneconomic Determinants of Nonmigration: Sociological Considerations for Migration Theory." *Rural Sociology* 38:296–311.

Ulrich, Martin A., and Wilbur R. Maki. 1973. *Financing Public Services in West Minnesota.* Minneapolis: Minnesota Agricultural Experiment Station Bulletin 509.

U.S. Bureau of the Census. 1972. *County and City Data Book.* Washington, D.C.: GPO.

———. 1975. *Historical Statistics of the United States, Colonial Times to 1970.* Washington, D.C.: GPO.

———. 1977. "Population Estimates and Projections: 1973 (revised) and 1975 Population Estimates and 1972 (revised) and 1974 Per Capita Income Estimates for Counties." *Current Population Reports.* Washington, D.C.: Department of Commerce, Bureau of the Census.

Voss, Paul B. 1980. "Turnaround Migration in the Upper Great Lakes Region." Paper presented at the Annual Meeting of the Population Association of America.

Wall Street Journal. 1981. "Branching Out." *The Wall Street Journal,* May 28.

Wardwell, J. M. 1977. "Equilibrium and Change in Nonmetropolitan Growth." *Rural Sociology* 42:156–179.

Wardwell, John M., and David L. Brown. 1980. "Population Redistribution in the United States during the 1970's." In *New*

Directions in Urban-Rural Migration, ed. David L. Brown and John M. Wardwell. New York: Academic Press.

Wardwell, John M., and C. Jack Gilchrist. 1978. "Metropolitan Change and Metropolitan Growth." Paper presented at the Annual Meeting of the Population Association of America, Atlanta, Georgia.

White, Fred, and Luther Tweeten. 1973. "Optimal School District Size Emphasizing Rural Areas." *Journal of Agricultural Economics* 55:45–53.

Yoesting, Dean R., and D. M. Marshall. 1969. "Trade Pattern Changes of Open Country Residents: A Longitudinal Study." *Rural Sociology* 34:85–101.

Zelinsky, Wilbur. 1962. "Changes in the Geographic Patterns of Rural Population in the United States 1790–1960." *The Geographical Review* 52:492–524.

———. 1978. "Is Nonmetropolitan America Being Repopulated? The Evidence from Pennsylvania's Minor Civil Divisions." *Demography* 15:13–39.

Zuiches, James J., and David L. Brown. 1978. "The Changing Character of the Nonmetropolitan Population, 1950–75." In *Rural U.S.A.: Persistence and Change,* ed. Thomas R. Ford. Ames: Iowa State University Press.

Zuiches, James J., and Glenn V. Fuguitt. 1972. "Residential Preferences: Implications for Population Redistribution in Nonmetropolitan Areas." In *Population Distribution and Policy,* ed. Sara Mills Mazie. Washington, D.C.: GPO.

Zuiches, James J., and Michael L. Price. 1980. "Industrial Dispersal and Labor-Force Migration: Employment Dimensions of the Population Turnaround in Michigan." In *New Directions in Urban-Rural Migration,* ed. David L. Brown and John M. Wardwell. New York: Academic Press.

Index

Adams, Bert N., 8, 10
Adjacency
  to metro areas, 34, 37, 112, 156
Age structure, 27–29
  and the turnaround, 109
Agriculture
  commercial, 8
  impact on demographic trends, 17, 29, 38, 39, 43, 126, 152
  mechanization of, 152
Amenities, 153
Anderson, A. H., 5, 8, 10, 12
Appalachia, 29, 32
Attitudes
  regarding nonmetro growth, 160

Baby boom
  end of, 107
  impact on demographic trends, 17, 24, 152
  See also Fertility
Beale, Calvin L., 6, 7, 18, 27, 29, 33, 37, 38, 39, 40, 44, 100, 106, 107, 112
Bender, Lloyd B., 77
Bias, simultaneity, 70, 98
Blacks, migration trends of, 23–24
Blue Ridge (Great Smokies), 33
Bollinger, W. Lamar, 6, 8, 11, 12, 45, 58
Bowles, Gladys K., 108
Brown, David L., 7, 11, 12, 39, 44, 99, 100, 109, 114, 115
Brunner, Edmund, 7

Business trends
  impact of economy on, 160
  in rural villages, 7
  See also Retail; Services
Buying power, 41, 126, 147. See also Consumer spending

Campbell, Rex R., 8, 9, 10, 11, 12, 37
Capital, retailing, 76, 154
Causal model
  procedures, 70
  for retailing, 47, 59–62
  for services, 85–88
  similarity of that for services and retailing, 95
Chain stores
  impact on local merchants, 10, 160
  increased demand for, 11
  in middle markets, 127
  in nonmetro areas, 8, 58, 76
Chang, H. C., 27, 107, 108
Change, irreversibility of, 161
Chicago, IL, 125
Cities. See Standard Metropolitan Statistical Areas
Cleveland, OH, 125
Clientele, in nonmetro stores, 127
Climate
  impact on population trends, 153
Coal fields, 29
Cohen, W., 22, 44
Competition, fear of, 10

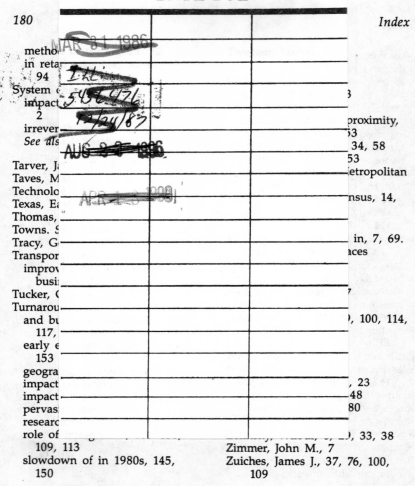